AINTREE'S QUEEN BEE

AINTREE'S QUEEN BEE

Joan Rimmer

SPORTS
BOOKS

Published by SportsBooks Ltd

Copyright: Joan Rimmer ©
September 2007

SportsBooks Limited
PO Box 422
Cheltenham
GL50 2YN
United Kingdom
Tel: 01242 256755
Fax: 01242 254694
e-mail   randall@sportsbooks.ltd.uk
Website   www.sportsbooks.ltd.uk

Cover designed by Alan Hunns

A CIP catalogue record for this book is available from the British Library.

ISBN 9781899807581
Printed by Creative Print and Design, Wales

I dedicate this book to all my friends who
have made life interesting.

Contents

ACKNOWLEDGEMENTS

This biography would not have been possible without the help, interest and collaboration of my friend James (Jim) Bidwell-Topham. Together we explored the life story of his extraordinary Aunt, Mirabel Dorothy Topham, the power behind the Grand National for almost half a century.

James, his sister Patricia and Mrs Topham bonded as 'The Topham Trio' and shared her encounters, adventures and experiences – some sad, some happy, others exciting, but never dull. This true and frank story has never been told and without Jim's help would have remained but a part of Aintree history, with the true wealth of the personality of the 'Queen Bee' buried in the past. Sadly my thanks to Jim are posthumous. He died on Thursday, November 18th 2005 aged 82.

My grateful thanks also to Jockey Club Racecourses and John Maxse, their director of communications, for their interest and assistance, Charles Barnett, former managing director of Aintree, now in a similar position at Ascot, and Bill Whittle, chairman of Haydock Park, for their valuable help and information.

I am indebted to Mary Hall and Christopher Hartley – Mary's husband Bill and Christopher – who are directly linked with John Davies the founder of Haydock racecourse, and Jean Bridge of the Hartley family. And to the recollections of my friends Brian and Ruth Moore with whom Jim Topham and I shared many happy times. I remember with gratitude the love and encouragement of my dear only sister Patricia Stroud, and my nieces Belinda and Amanda who live in California and that of my goddaughter Julie Barraclough. I appreciate the interest of Peter Dimmock and his daughter Amanda.

Jim Topham would have wanted me to thank on his behalf the Rimmer family – my niece Joan Bangor-Jones, husband Richard, and sons David and Charles – for their friendship and kindness. Remembering the happy occasions we all shared together during the Christmas festivities which helped to alleviate some of his loneliness after the deaths of his aunt and sister.

Finally I would like to express my greatest debt of gratitude to my friends Carolyn Bass and Janet Boyle for their computer expertise in helping me to prepare this manuscript. As a devotee of a manual typewriter myself their assistance has been invaluable.

PHOTOGRAPH ACKNOWLEDGEMENTS

I would like to thank Charlotte Bird on behalf of her late uncle for the use of the 'Russians at Aintree' photographs taken by Medley and Bird, New Brighton and Wallasey photographers.

PROLOGUE

It was at the 2007 Grand National meeting that the curtain finally came down with a theatrical flourish on the extraordinary story of Mirabel Dorothy Topham, the former actress who masterminded the world's most famous steeplechase for almost half a century, and thereby concluded the Topham family's 159-year association with Aintree racecourse.

The unfolding drama centred on Paddock Lodge, Mirabel's much loved residence for 48 years, formerly the Topham Company's offices and the only house on the racecourse.

At the start of the three-day Grand National meeting, a green plastic banner approximately 10ft x 3ft emblazoned in white with the words 'House for Sale' was suspended on its frontage to inform the world at large that Mirabel's former home was on the market – price tagged at £1,250,000.

Upstairs in what had been her film-star-size pink bedroom the estate agent from the upmarket Knight Frank, who were handling the sale, sat at his desk and offered an inspection of the house to any interested racegoers who might fancy living there. There had been an earlier attempt at a much-needed makeover to improve the appearance of the house, which had fallen into a sad state of disrepair. The leaking roof through which rain had dripped had been replaced and a team of painters had coated the window frames with a quick fix of undercoat. Holes scooped out of the front lawn held water-filled jam jars containing daffodils and spring flowers. But it was thanks to the superb reorganisation of Aintree racecourse by the Jockey Club Racecourses that Paddock Lodge was ensured of a prime location a few yards from the rails of the magnificent new parade ring and winners' enclosure with an unrivalled viewpoint from the upstairs bay window from which to survey the runners and riders, their owners and trainers. A vantage point much appreciated by the estate agent when he sited his desk!

The sale of such an important part of Aintree history had been stage-managed to perfection under the spotlight of brilliant spring sunshine by the new owner – Nicholas Ryan, a retired investment banker and the great-great-grandson of Edward William Topham, who had negotiated the lease of Aintree racecourse from Lord Sefton in 1848. Nicholas Ryan had timed the sale to coincide with the three-day Grand National meeting, knowing full well that the television cameras filming the action in the parade ring and winners' enclosure would include a viewing of Paddock Lodge and the huge 'For Sale' banner to a world-wide television audience. He persuaded Clare Balding, the star of BBC's racing coverage, to interview him and tour the house on the second day of TV coverage. There was wide press coverage linking up with the Aintree festival.

Aintree's 'Queen Bee' had always enjoyed a good show and being the centre of attention. It was part of her theatrical indoctrination and had remained with her throughout her life. Whether or not she would have approved of that current spectacle is a matter of conjecture... particularly as the hub of the action appeared to be directed from her boudoir! Although I suspect that she might have had a hint of admiration for Nicholas and his brilliant timing and marketing strategy to obtain the highest offer for his great-aunt's 'Jewel in the Crown'. He had, indeed, proved himself to be a chip off the old block.

After Mirabel's death in 1980, her nephew James Bidwell-Topham had lived in Paddock Lodge until his death in 2005. It had then passed on to Nicholas Ryan who, at the time of writing, lives in Wiltshire with his South African wife.

The house was the last piece of the Aintree racecourse not owned by Jockey Club Racecourses. It had been widely expected that they would buy this once impressive and historical building and either restore it to its former status, worthy of taking its place on the famous racecourse, or use the valuable site and adjacent land for an extension of their programme of reorganisation. It was not an attractive prospect that an outside buyer could purchase the last important piece of Aintree within their grasp.

Nicholas's secret plan to project the sale of Paddock Lodge under the same spotlight as the world's most important steeplechase had taken both Jockey Club Racecourses and the Aintree Racecourse Company by surprise. There had been no preliminary dialogue to give Jockey Club Racecourses the opportunity to negotiate their interest.

It was not until the first day of the Grand National meeting that they became aware that the house was on the open market and the full extent of the vendor's initiative in stage-managing its sale. In fact the dialogue did not begin until after the Grand National meeting had ended by which time Nicholas held the ace, having already established an ambitious purchase price, fanned the publicity and attracted considerable outside interest.

Mirabel loved her home in the heart of the racecourse. She had excluded it from the sale of Aintree to Bill Davies in 1973 so that it would always be her permanent residence.

Paddock Lodge had been the hub of her life there – office, command post and a place of escapism from the world outside. The red brick walls also concealed some skeletons in her closet. Mirabel was always an actress, in control, with an abundance of confidence, charm and joviality, guaranteed to give a star performance. Few people ever penetrated this façade which would have revealed times of unhappiness and having to cope with the trials and tribulations of marital disharmony.

She was a woman of remarkable strength and character and it was a fortunate day for Arthur Ronald Topham when he married the beautiful actress – not only for himself but also for the future of the Grand National.

There is little doubt that had she not taken the reins from her inadequate and fallible husband the future of the world's most famous steeplechase would have been in jeopardy.

He created many problems which she managed with fortitude based on a philosophy revealed in a few lines penned by her on 'The Grand National Steeplechase':

The Charm of this Chase is its so like life,
Needing Courage, Skill and how to dodge strife.

Mirabel Dorothy Topham's story has never been told although she said on a number of occasions that she planned to write her memoirs.

Mirabel, her niece Pat and nephew Jim, were my friends for 37 years and their story, including many of their anecdotal recollections, is one I write with affection.

So it was in 2007 the last spiritual presence of Aintree's Queen Bee took flight into the annals of history. Or did she? One lady visitor viewing within Mirabel's bedroom turned pale and made a hurried exit, saying she felt an 'icy cold, overpowering presence'.

CHAPTER ONE

MIRABEL ON STAGE

Mirabel Dorothy Topham, chairman of Aintree racecourse for more than 40 years, knew nothing about the sport before her marriage in 1922 to Arthur Ronald Topham.

Indeed, her closest encounter with a horse was as an actress in a theatrical production when she rode on stage clinging to the mane of an elderly mare called Daisy, hoping she would not fall off.

Little did she realise at the time that in due course destiny would guide her into the role of leading lady of the world's greatest steeplechase, the Grand National, and that it would be her shrewd business management that would ensure the continuation of its success as Britain's greatest sporting event, not that of her inadequate, erring husband.

As first lady of the course she would control 270 acres including 59 acres of racecourse, 274 stables, public accommodation, stands, fences and their maintenance, and an eight-acre farm. Twelve families lived on the course and she would manage a staff of 40 – increasing in number as the National meeting drew nigh.

Mirabel, the eldest of four children, was born on August 7th 1891, at the Barons Court Hotel, Comeragh Road, on the West Kensington side of Fulham, where she spent her childhood. The family lived together with her grandparents James Hillier, a licensed victualler, who managed the hotel, his wife Rachel, and Mirabel's parents. Harry Hillier, who worked as the assistant licensed victualler, his wife Nellie, and James Hillier's 18-year-old niece, Emily Godding, who filled in as barmaid.

At the age of 20, Harry – or Henry Hope Hillier as he preferred to be called – had eloped to marry pretty 19-year-old Nellie Buck with whom he was madly in love, after her parents, who lived at St Albans, had refused to give their consent, considering him completely unsuitable and with no financial prospects. Mirabel's father, who was born in Lambeth, told her that on one of the few occasions he met his future father-in-law, he had put out his hand and said; 'How do you do, Sir.' Mr Buck deliberately put his hands behind his back, bowed and said 'How do you do,' but refused to shake hands. A tearful Nellie implored her parents to agree to the marriage and give them their blessing. They refused and the result was that neither Mirabel nor her brother and sisters ever met their maternal grandparents.

The Hillier family existed on limited means but were blessed with an abundance of affection. Mirabel, her sister Beatrice and brother Cedric – another sister died in infancy – all enjoyed a happy carefree childhood in a loving home and she described her parents as being a 'honeymoon couple all their lives'.

She was to tell me: 'My birthright was neither money nor a title, but an excellent constitution and for that I am exceedingly thankful.'

This held true for the rest of the family. Both Cedric and Beatrice lived into their nineties and Mirabel died in her eighty-ninth year.

In later years, Mirabel often explored the memories of a 'very happy childhood' and told her nephew Jim and his sister Pat: 'I was blessed in my gift of origin and could not have chosen better parents, whose depth of love and understanding surpassed the requirements of parental responsibility. They created for my sister, brother and I, a safe and happy environment. We had a caring, stable and loving home and were encouraged to explore and to achieve every opportunity that came along.'

They were further blessed with the additional affection and care of their paternal grandparents with whom they lived. The atmosphere at the Baron's Court Hotel was friendly and sociable and Mirabel learned at an early age to be a good mixer with those in all walks of life. It was useful groundwork for a future role as Aintree's 'Queen Bee', and there is little doubt that the combination of charm, sociability and the need, as a child, to dominate would eventually make her a star of some show or other.

She was exceedingly pretty and close friends and family called her 'Mirrie'. From an early age she was organised and would tidy away and store her toys and books so that they were immediately to hand when needed. At school she was a top-grade pupil, excelling in English, arithmetic and sport.

In later years her niece, Pat, was amused when her Aunt told her that as a child she could be quite bossy and liked to be the organiser. Apparently the other children respected this and never queried her childlike authority so there were few arguments and scraps. She enjoyed being the leader and was never short of an opinion nor lacked the courage to express it. She had inherited this strength from her father who was a strong-minded man in all his dealings. It was he who angrily came to her aid when the 'unacceptable behaviour of Ronald' caused him and the parish priest to suggest they end their engagement.

It mattered little to him that Ronald Topham was a member of the famous racecourse family – telling him bluntly in a letter: 'Regarding any money you might or might not have, I would prefer my daughter to marry a man who could earn his living.'

Mirrie adored both of her parents and they instilled in her the need to succeed – as was so often illustrated in many of the inspirational poetic words she penned along the way.

This was apparent in her gift of a poem to her goddaughter Amanda Dimmock, the last verse reading:

Whatever you aim at – go in with Zest
And make sure always to give of your best
Then if you should lose just lose with a smile.
Counting the effort an effort worthwhile!

As children and teenagers, Mirabel and her brother and sister were encouraged to keep busy and have an appetite for life. They fenced, swam, rowed on the Thames, where there was a female rowing club, walked and cycled for miles in the wealth of local parks providing attractive recreational facilities for everyone, and they still had the energy to dance the hours away.

Idleness was not in the family curriculum and as a result the children – the girls in particular – progressed into self-reliant teenagers, qualities which in the years to come would provide a winning combination for the future 'Queen Bee', and give her the strength to cope with a frequently inebriated and at times violent husband.

Their father was a talented artist and more interested in the aesthetic side of art than in making money out of his creative talent. His interests included the theatre and when an opportunity was offered for him to become manager of the Haymarket Theatre he was delighted to accept. This job and his close theatrical connections inspired both Mirabel and her sister to decide in their teens on a stage career. Mirabel, as Hope Hillier, became an actress and Beatrice, as Trixie Hillier, a Gaiety Girl, both appearing in West End productions.

Mirabel's first introduction to the limelight was as an eight-year-old schoolgirl, when, at her father's request, she helped out by filling in a small role in a Haymarket production and was rewarded with a bag of sweets, her father pocketing the small fee.

The girls had inherited their mother's beauty and stature, and it was a natural progression in that era for young ladies of great charm and comeliness – if opportunity came their way – to follow a theatrical career.

At the turn of the century the standards for the stage were exacting. At the Gaiety the qualifications for even a member of the chorus were appearance, the skill to move gracefully, and the ability to sing tunefully. A better class of girl soon entered this circuit and the standard of talent and intelligence was then at its highest. The music of the day required singing par excellence, with the essential combination of good looks and grace.

The show girls and their admirers proved a positive asset to the Gaiety's profits, for those were the days when wealthy young men and the aristocracy mingled with 'Stage Door Johnnies' to book their stall seats and boxes regularly for several nights a week, for the run of the performance.

Letters of admiration, requests for photographs and autographs poured in with gifts of chocolates and flowers. The hopeful suitors would hang around the stage door, resplendent in full evening dress – topper, white kid gloves, white waistcoat and the rest – in the hope they would be allowed to escort one of the theatre ladies to a champagne supper.

They were often lucky and the ladies would disappear

with a swish of silk into a hansom cab in a haze of perfume and cigar smoke.

The future generation of the peerage lay in the Gaiety chorus with the union of scions of ancient lineage and the good looking young women who decorated the theatre's boards. Many of the alliances were successful, for the Gaiety girl, as a rule, was a woman of sophistication, possessing tact and intelligence which helped when adapting to her new surroundings. Indeed, the Gaiety girl turned peeress proved an asset to her new position and she was well able to cope in spite of gloomy predictions from pessimistic dowagers and those in high society.

Hope and Trixie Hillier were already the toast of the various gallants of the day. In her seventies, Mirabel was still a very handsome woman and in her younger days was a great beauty, although Trixie was even more beautiful. It is not difficult to understand why Arthur Ronald Topham, himself a stage door Johnny, was bowled over at their first meeting.

Arthur, a World War I private in the Royal Artillery, had been interested in the theatre since his teenage years and in particular the lovely girls who graced the stage. He enjoyed a pastime of trawling the theatres, ogling the stage beauties and weaving pipe dreams about the availability and joy of their company.

Both Mirabel and her sister had successful careers. Mirabel perfected prominent roles at such London theatres as the Vaudeville on the Strand and the Empire Theatre, Leicester Square, and had toured with leading London companies which included famous actors such as Jack Hulbert, Cicely Courtneidge and Fay Compton. She appeared with George Edwardes in several pieces at the Gaiety Theatre.

In 1922 at the time of her marriage to Ronald – as she

preferred to call him – she was on stage playing in *Quality Street* at the Haymarket Theatre, London. She had also taken principal parts in pantomime.

Although frequently described in the press as a 'Gaiety Girl', Mirabel was in fact a talented actress of repute and in June 1907 had a role in a Three Acts farce *Mrs Ponderburys Past*, at the Vaudeville. It was a highly amusing play with good lines and beautiful costumes and was produced under the direction of Mr Charles Hawtrey (later Sir Charles) a leading actor-producer of great distinction who had managed 16 theatres in London and put on more than 100 plays. He selected only the most reputable of actresses and taking part with Mirabel in *Mrs Ponderburys Past* was Billie Burke who later starred in New York and Hollywood and became Mrs Florenz Ziegfield of 'Follies' fame.

Over the years, Ronald had been collecting photographs of Trixie, but decided instead to pursue her sister and asked a friend to arrange an introduction. She was appearing in a London Show called *The Cinema Star*, a musical comedy, which had been hastily transferred to the old Royal Court Theatre, Liverpool, following an attack by the press on its German composer Jean Gilbert, who had been born Max Waterfield in Hamburg.

Ronald had booked a seat in the stalls several nights running to admire the 'Girls' – Hope in particular – enjoy the music, the comedy, and in particular the duet 'Oh Louisa', sung by a bevy of lovely Cinema Girls:

Oh Louisa, the world is at your feet!
Oh Louisa, your triumph is complete!
Any man you please goes upon his knees to Louisa,
    Louisa, Louisa!

The actresses were all exquisitely gowned and Hope described in the press as a 'true type of Saxon Beauty' – with her azure blue eyes and wavy fair hair burnished like gold, wore a taffeta gown of blue appliquéd in silver and a net tunic fastened with a large pink rose. In another spectacular scene the Cinema company featured harem girls, shepherd and shepherdesses galore. In all it was a brilliant production.

Ronald rose to his feet to applaud enthusiastically as the company assembled for the final bow, before hot-footing it to the stage door to intercept Hope and invite her out for supper. 'It was all such good fun,' he told her as they sipped champagne and he gazed in admiration into her twinkling blue eyes.

It was the start of a courtship culminating in their engagement in 1916 and marriage, six years later. However, the road of true love did not run smoothly, mainly due to Ronald's mercurial inconsistency and wavering en route to the altar. His emotional instability was of great concern to Mirabel's father, their parish priest and friends. Their disquiet is illustrated in letters sent at the time of their betrothal.

Ronald was in the army for most of the years of courtship and for months on end they corresponded by letter. His family were disappointed that he wished to remain as Private Topham and did not accept his stripe of promotion which would have suggested at least a hint of ambition!

On leave he visited the theatres where Mirabel was performing, travelling to the provinces when she was on tour. They dined with friends. Mirabel, with her bright personality, sense of fun and the talent to tell an amusing story she knew would entertain all present, was in great demand. Her fiancée tagged along, enjoying the hospitality to which he suddenly found himself included. His friends puzzled as to how he had managed to win such a personable and attractive woman.

His letters at times were hurtful, critical and full of unjustified suspicions reflecting his own character weaknesses and uncertainty.

Mirabel's parents cared deeply for their children. It was a mutual bond of love that remained steadfast throughout their lives and when a tearful Mirabel showed her father the current letter she had received from Ronald on her birthday, full of mischievous and noxious comments, Mr Hillier was enraged and determined that his daughter should not be troubled further by a man he considered a 'cad' and wrote him the following letter.

Dear Ronald

I trust when you return to London again you will not worry Mirrie with your attentions any more. She was well and happy when you came back but you deliberately sought her out, made all sorts of promises and finally got her to wear her ring and promise to be a good wife. Then you go away and write such a letter as she has received today (her Birthday). What I think of you is unutterable and if you have a grain of gentlemanly feeling in you at all what must you think of yourself? As a parent you can hardly expect me to calmly stand by and see my daughter played fast and loose with as you have done these last few years. So please let this matter end here. Myself and all who know her think as I do, that she is worthy of a better and more steadfast affection than you seem capable of giving, and as regards any money you may or may not have, it is not an asset that counts in our family as we should much prefer to see Mirrie married to a man who could earn a living.

Mirrie has promised both Father Dyer and myself to try
and think no more about you and I trust you will also
regard my wishes in this matter.
Hillier

The seriousness and the possible consequences of the
letter caused Ronald to try and make amends for the
harshness of his attitude towards Mirabel. In his heart he
did not want to lose her but there were certain aspects
of his personality – which their life together would later
reveal – that were beyond his control.

He also experienced pangs of jealousy towards the
many admirers of her talent and celebrity status who
showered her with flowers, cards and compliments. This
was illustrated in a letter he wrote in 1916:

Dearest Mirrie
It was awfully nice of you to come down to the station and
see me off. You are a wonderful plucky little girl and kept
up your spirits fine (perhaps though you have someone
else in your eye to cheer you up which may accord for
your cheery spirits!! Keep steadfast to old Ron (if you can)
love and kisses.

Mirabel accepted all homage with good grace but she
was always absolutely faithful to Ronald.

Her fan mail was impressive, particularly from
war weary troops in WWI, and she willingly sent her
photograph in response to servicemen enduring the
horrors of battle. Her brother Cedric fought throughout
the Gallipoli campaign and she had a special and loyal
affection for the troops.

Not all the cards were of hearts and flowers, and
affectionate regards. Some illustrated the love of country

and national spirit of the sender. One such card was sent in 1916 by a Sergeant Major H Thompson addressed: 'With kindly greetings to Miss Mirabel Hillier.' On it was a stirring patriotic verse surrounded by groups of flag-bearing soldiers under the shield of the honorary Artillery Company and their motto *Arma Pacis Fulcra* – 'armed strength for peace'.

The verse read:

Where is the slave who of England despairing
Aids not her cause when she summons her sons?
Where is the knave who when foemen are daring
Parleys for safety, or crouches and runs?
England neer grew them!
Her soil never knew them;
Wholesomes the earth in our isle of the sea.
Our maidens would flout them:
Our children would scout them.
Wed hoot them with scorn from our land of the free!

Mirabel found this inspiring and kept it for the rest of her life.

The fall-out from Mr Hillier's letter of rebuke caused a breach in her engagement during which Mirabel allowed Charlie, a friend of Ronald's, to be her companion. Ronald immediately took it upon himself to write to Charlie and tell him that the engagement was on again.

He wrote to Mirabel from No. 14 Camp, BEF on December 3rd 1916:

Dear Mirrie
I agree with Father Dyer that I cannot phone you if you get engaged to anyone else while on your tour. Over that

you can please yourself but I shall know then that you care for me no more. Of course, don't fail to let me know if you do. I have written to Charlie and told him that our engagement is on again and we hope to complete the happy event on my return. Well as we are off in 15 minutes – I must close.
Love Ronnie xxxx

It was not the sort of letter of which romantic dreams are made but it seemed to have worked. Upon his return they made up and the engagement was officially on again.

There were those who thought Ronald would benefit from the harsh reality of life on the front line.

A close family friend, recovering from his wounds in St James Military Hospital, Liverpool, wrote on November 28th 1916.

Dear Mirrie
Thank you very much for your welcome letter. Of course when I last wrote to you I had no idea Ronald had gone to France. It was a great surprise. Mrs Topham wrote and told me, and I have since heard from Ronald. He is training at the base, so of course it might be quite a time before he actually gets to the fighting line! It does every man good to know what it is to rough it. Everyone tells me I look better than I ever did before. I am sure it will do Ronald good, he has had such an easy life so far. At the front you learn what hunger and thirst are about, and money is almost no use to you, so it makes you appreciate the good things when you can have them.
Cheer up Mirrie, the war cannot last forever and I trust it will not be very long before I am present at your wedding.

This hospital is strict. I can only get out two hours in the morning and two hours in the afternoon and we have to be in by four o'clock. I must be thankful I am still alive. I met a man last week who was with me in the 24th Battalion at Northampton, and he told me that there were only seventeen men left out of the 16th Battalion (the one I was with in France). I do know that the poor 16th no longer exists.

I am sure the pantomime at Leeds, will be a big success with your beauty and talent – so here's to success. I will have to drink the toast another time as there is nothing here but medicines.

Cheerio Gerard

There was another letter addressed to Miss Hillier, Vaudeville Theatre, Strand, from Guy, Suffolk Yeomanry, Essex October 11th 1916 on the occasion of her engagement.

My dear Mirrie

Just a few lines to congratulate you and wish you oh such lots of happiness. I am glad you are happy now – Still, somehow I think you are not quite so happy as you ought to be – Maybe I am wrong. Hope not. Good bye Mirrie. Guy.

Mirabel's sister Beatrice married in August 1918 to James Ross of Epsom. It was a very happy marriage and produced two children, Valerie and Donald.

James Ross was away on business and wrote:

Dear Mirrie

I am sorry I cannot be at your wedding on Wednesday. However, I shall be there in thought. I am so glad that everything has come right in the end. I am sure, that you

*must love Ronald very much and that you will be very
happy. I know that you can be very charming if you want
to and since you have given your love to Ronald it will
please you to make him happy and as love begets love,
Ronald should not fail in making your marriage a joyous
one. The very best I can wish you both is that you will
be as happy and content with married life as I am with
Trixie and our daughter.*
Love Jimmy

A letter from a priest described to them:

*The power of conjugal love is the devotion of a man to his
wedded wife —and a wife to her loyal husband. I have seen it
many times and know that it is the strongest thing to hold
one fast to each other. Love of wealth, power and luxury,
are dependent on things visible and temporal, and when
these are made inaccessible their desire ceases. But the true
love of husband and wife are of the soul and dies only with
it, or dies not at all, being changeless and eternal.*

The marriage announcement appeared in *The Times* on
Friday April 28th 1922.

*TOPHAM – HOPE HILLIER. On the 19th April, at
Our Lady and St Edward, Chiswick, A. Ronald Topham,
of York House, Kensington, to Mirabel Dorothy, daughter
of Mr and Mrs Hope Hillier, of Priory Road, Bedford
Park, London.*

A Mayfair manufacturer of wedding dresses designed
the elegant slim-line gown of cream cloque with leg
of mutton sleeves, and a fitted waistline to enhance the
bride's shapely figure. Matching shoes peeped out from

below the hemline and her filmy tulle veil was held in place by a headband of flowers. She held a spray of white arum lilies with trailing stephanotis and radiated beauty and happiness.

On the marriage certificate, Arthur Ronald Topham is described as a 36-year-old bachelor of independent means. Mirabel Dorothy Hillier a 30-year-old spinster – rank or profession left blank.

Another friend wrote:

It was a really beautiful ceremony – most devotional and wholly Catholic. I cannot tell you what a pleasure it was to me to see Ronald so happily settling down in life.

Mirabel's parents hosted a generous reception after which the newlyweds left for a honeymoon at the Lynton Cottage Hotel, in North Devon, staying eight days for a total cost of £30 19s 4d. In 2005, based on average earnings, that was worth around £5,000.

To keep out the seafront chill Mirabel took with her the new Russian sable stole she had purchased for £212 from a Highbury furrier.

The Catholic Association had arranged a pilgrimage to Rome which left London on May 18th 1922 – a journey Mirabel and Ronald had particularly wanted to join. This was arranged and they enjoyed two nights at the Hotel Flora in Rome and two nights at the Hotel Suisse in Turin before returning home.

During the early years of their marriage, Ronald and Mirabel divided their time between Aintree, and their home in Warwickshire where they lived with their two fox terriers Frisky and Frolic. In Warwickshire, Mirabel worked tirelessly for charities. At one time she was connected, in a practical way, with ten. One of her favourites was 'Moral Welfare' and the plight of the unmarried mother. She devoted her time and energy to counselling and sorting out the many problems which faced the one-parent family in those less tolerant days when help so desperately needed was unavailable at official level. She had always been well possessed with good sound common sense and her workable solutions and financial assistance helped many a girl on the threshold of the workhouse to avoid admittance. In addition she was chairman of the Birmingham Archdiocese Catholic Women's League.

Her organisational skills were also used to help in the production of the Earl of Warwick's pageant in July 1930 when her father's interest in history and art provided authentic information, including that for the clothes which were precisely fashioned on the period.

There was much acclamation for her efforts which had been time consuming and as a result Mirabel blamed herself for Frisky, one of her fox terriers, catching a cold and dying. She was so upset by his demise that the organisers presented her with a replacement which she called Beecham and this was her first Scottie dog.

The Sea Scouts, the Pony Club, theatre and boxing charities, Animal Welfare, shire horses and help for children and the elderly – all received her support and generous financial help.

At the age of 26, she had completed a car maintenance course and could dismantle and reassemble a vehicle engine with ease. She had received her driving licence in March 1915.

Her other interests included domestic science and in particular cooking. She was herself a brilliant cook and encouraged all young women to become proficient in culinary skills. She taught young hard-up housewives how to transform a couple of pounds of scrag-end, carrots, onion and potatoes, into an appetising meal for the family at very low cost. In later life she was puzzled why young women spent to excess on ready-made processed foods when there was such a variety of nourishing vegetables and cheap pieces of meat available to satisfy family appetites.

The Topham family had lived for some centuries at East Witton in Yorkshire, as tenant farmers on land owned by the Earls of Ailesbury. Their family tree could be traced back to 1636 the eleventh year of the reign of King Charles 1st, when Edward Topham farmed there.

The inspiration for the creation of the Topham dynasty at Aintree, came from the initiative of Edward William Topham, Ronald's grandfather.

Edward, famous for his knowledge of horses, moved from Middleham, Yorkshire, in 1830 to Chester, to revive the racecourse there which was having limited success. In 1837 he was clerk of the course and handicapper there.

Thirty miles away the Aintree Syndicate was also in difficulties and Edward, a shrewd businessman, was sufficiently interested in the long-term possibilities of Aintree, to continue his strategic planning to take over the lease of the Liverpool racecourse.

His vision led to an earlier purchase of several acres of land adjoining Warbreck Moor and when he did take over the lease of the course from Lord Sefton in 1848, he built stables on it. Fired with enthusiasm, he left the management of Chester to his sons, Christopher Reuben and Joseph Bell while he concentrated all his time and energy on Aintree, although they later followed him there.

It was Edward who framed the handicap for the first Grand National run under these conditions, then known as the Grand National steeplechase. Steeped in tradition and rich human interest, the Grand National presented a thrilling and colourful spectacle of courageous riders and stout-hearted horses contesting the biggest steeple-chasing obstacles in the world. There is no doubt that it was the acumen of Edward William Topham which made it a British institution.

Joseph Bell Topham, who later took on the duties of handicapper of the Grand National from his father, had, as his personal secretary, his middle son Arthur Ronald, but it was his eldest son Edward Anthony Christopher who took over the handicapping of the 'Chase' on the death of his father.

EAC Topham held the reins of Tophams Ltd, for 28 years, with considerable success both at home and abroad, but towards the end of his time he began to lose heart. After his death in 1932 there was a conflict of family and business interests and the appointment of Arthur Ronald Topham as Aintree chief was greeted with dismay. Many people in the racing world, aware of Ronald's lack of moral strength and business initiative, doubted he would be able to cope with such important responsibilities. Sadly Ronald had inherited few of the capable and stable genes of his clever Yorkshire grandfather or his business flair.

Arthur Ronald was politely known as a genial 'Peter Pan', a 'happy-go-lucky ' man but in reality he was often irresponsible, and drank to excess, fuelling his violent and aggressive tendencies. It was his lucky day when he married Mirabel, his steadfast and capable bride, to help him over the hurdles.

There had been a few examples of his irresponsibility and lack of consideration during their lengthy courtship and in retrospect it is hard to understand how such a perceptive woman as Mirabel remained unaware or chose to ignore, that her future husband was a man of so many imperfections. After periods of binge drinking, his ill-temper often exploded into uncontrollable rage and physical abuse. He would later reveal another disturbing tendency – to disappear into the night in search of other company. Perhaps Mirabel thought she could control him. Being a powerful influence was her forte and there was no way the future 'Iron Lady' of Aintree would allow herself to become a battered wife, or indeed, for that matter, a submissive one. Or maybe she was an optimist. She considered it a lucky omen when the horse *Music Hall* won at her first Grand National meeting in 1922.

CHAPTER TWO

TAKING THE REINS AT AINTREE

It was remarkable for a woman to rise to the top in this era. Mirabel, a pioneer in a man's world, joined the company in 1934, became a director in 1935, and, in due course, with determination and ability, propelled herself into the role of chairman and managing director. Her husband was more than satisfied to remain the 'happy-go-lucky' figure in the background, leaving his immensely capable wife to manage the family business.

An example of male opposition to women in high office is illustrated in the history of Haydock racecourse, which was started in 1898 on land leased from Lord Newton by John Davies. At the time of his death, Davies left all his shares in Haydock racecourse to his granddaughter Dolly. She married Sydney Sandon, a clerk and office accountant, who first became secretary of Haydock racecourse and later managing director and chairman.

It was presumed that Dolly, having inherited the shares, would become a member of the board. Sydney Sandon refused to allow this because 'she is a woman'.

Mirabel, their racecourse neighbour and close friend of the family, was furious at such disrespect for both her sex and Dolly. She tackled Sandon at a dinner party: 'Tell me Sydney, why is Dolly not on the board?' He told her bluntly: 'I don't approve of women on the board,' and refused to discuss the matter further. Mirabel ignored him for the rest of the evening and never forgave him for his prejudicial attitude.

It was soon obvious that Mirabel's ascent, in what had always been considered a male province, was rapidly rising to command position. It was not about proving herself as a strong woman in a male dominated world. She was never a radical feminist, considering that energy channelled into resentment clouded vision and ambition. Her qualities had been established in childhood by parents who had occupied every minute of her time with constructive thoughts and activities to keep her fully occupied and to stretch her both mentally and physically.

She championed the world's greatest steeplechase from the heart, moving forward, alert and sharp-witted. She was a keen businesswoman and a human dynamo of energy. She was noted for plain speaking, frequently criticised and at times even disliked by her opponents, but still they all respected her.

For in as much as her forthrightness and frankness of words might have upset or angered the people with whom she dealt they knew precisely where they stood. She was direct and honest and would never go back on her word.

Her ideas caused consternation and anger in some quarters and she admitted on occasions being in dispute with the Jockey Club and that outside trainers showed resentment towards her.

However, members of the Jockey Club were always happy to accept an invitation to enjoy the excellence of her luncheon hospitality. After one particular generous lunch at Paddock Lodge, during which a Jockey Club guest had enjoyed a second helping of roast beef, Mirabel was amused when he turned to her, raised his glass in salutation and said, 'Mrs Topham, I cannot agree with a word you have uttered but by Jove I cannot fault the succulence of your roast beef!'

'The Iron Lady' of Aintree's battles were often in the

headlines but wartime censorship prevented the revelation of one of her most interesting victories.

At the outbreak of war in 1939, racing was brought to a standstill and Mirabel piloted the racecourse through its first occupation by troops in September. She helped with their quick departure early in the following year in time to stage the 1940 Grand National Meeting. The late Lord Derby, on behalf of the racing authorities, was greatly impressed with her achievement, congratulating and thanking her for 'giving the country a tonic in its hour of need'.

With the fall of France the racecourse was again quickly occupied and over-run by 16,000 troops of many nationalities and a wide range of accompanying vehicles. Senior officers were billeted at Paddock Lodge and in the stands, while troops were lodged in Nissen huts erected within the racecourse boundary. Mirabel, her husband, and their niece, Pat Bidwell-Topham, lived at Paddock Lodge and Mirabel was able to keep a close eye on matters concerning the racecourse. Their nephew James was himself in the Army for part of that time.

She monitored the troop's influx and the care of the course like a General and when the Commanding Officer informed her that the War Office intended to erect concrete blocks along the length of the course to prevent the landing of German planes, she was horrified and refused permission, saying it would ruin the racecourse. Correspondence raged between the War Office and Mirabel. A personal appeal by a senior officer, despatched to Aintree from the War Office, was to no avail. Eventually, the War Office yielded to her objection and Aintree remained a hazard-free landing strip for enemy planes. Perhaps had the Germans ever arrived the War Office could have used Mirabel as their secret weapon.

She surprised the racing authorities again with the speed by which she was able to again clear out the troops in February 1946 and stage the post-war 'National' less than two months after their departure. Lord Rosebery expressed his amazement at the quantities of equipment that had been rediscovered and renewed at that difficult time.

To Mirabel it was no surprise. She had made sure that a quantity of important items of racecourse equipment had been hidden away to remain undiscovered until the war ended. This piece of enterprise helped the 1946 Grand National to get off to a flying start.

Paddock Lodge, less than half-a-mile from where the horses parade for the Grand National, had been a derelict timbered town cottage, originally the registered offices of Tophams Ltd. Before that it had contained the luncheon rooms of the Duke of Westminster and other celebrated racing enthusiasts. It was condemned to be pulled down about the time that Mirabel joined the company in 1934. She spotted its possibilities and under her supervision the cottage was more or less gutted and extended into a superior two-storey rustic brick house she appropriately called 'Paddock Lodge', and it became the Topham's Aintree residence.

Previously, they had rented a flat in Sefton Park, Liverpool, as a temporary abode. It irritated Mirabel, a workaholic, that by the time they arrived for work at the racecourse each day Ronald would look at his watch and say, 'Come on missus, time for lunch.' They would have a four shillings and sixpenny lunch at the Exchange Hotel before returning to work. Mirabel told him it was such a waste of time and decided that Paddock Lodge should become their permanent home.

Her haven of peace and time for quiet reflection after

a full day of unstinting work or the fall-out of Ronald's tantrums was the sitting room, a restful, comfortable place, with an abundance of flowers and plants, which faced the racecourse.

On one wall was a superb Ben Herring watercolour of a top-hatted starter with a field of jockeys ready for 'off'. When the sun streamed into the room it illuminated the magnificent colours of the jockeys' silks and the gloss on the coats of their thoroughbred mounts.

On the ground floor, the 28ft boardroom was used on occasions as a reception area for entertaining and had sliding doors leading to the dining room. The windows, draped in white tulle, overlooked the Parade Ring. Also on the ground floor were a large kitchen, a pantry, laundry room, sewing room, the accountant's office, a handyman's storage area and a large cloakroom.

On the second floor, Mirabel's elegant, pale pink bedroom, spanning 28ft, had star quality and was obviously designed for a lady of distinction. The dressing table was of theatrical size dimensions and topped with a splendid three-sided mirror. There was an en suite bathroom and dressing room, and also on that floor were four more bedrooms and two bathrooms.

In spring, and for the Grand National meeting, the surrounding garden was carpeted with a multitude of daffodils and spring flowers. A high wall ensured privacy and protected the house from the noise and rush of the traffic on the main road outside.

Even after she sold the racecourse, Mirabel refused to sever completely her links with Aintree and she lived at Paddock Lodge until her death in 1980.

She owned three other homes. Two were at Seaview on the Isle of Wight, overlooking the Solent. One, West Ingle, a large graceful residence of character was set high amid trees and rolling lawns, and below, in the lower part of its two-tiered garden, was a smaller extended dormer-type bungalow she had adapted for her own convenience and comfort. A gate from the garden opened onto their private pathway to the beach below. This is where 'I recharge my batteries,' she told me.

At Seaview Mirabel had the status among the local community equal in lustre and prestige to that of the Queen Bee of Aintree racecourse. She was known as an organiser of merit who could solve any problems, no matter what, and get things done. Consequently a number of local difficulties – such as the erosion of the sea wall – usually finished up at her front door.

She was happy to enter into battle with anyone on behalf of local residents. The local council had long learned that Mrs Topham was no pushover and would fight them to the last line of any official directive if she so disagreed. The sea wall in question was at the end of her garden, and she and her neighbours were rightly worried about sea erosion. In winter when gales swept the sea beyond, the wall was constantly battered by the pounding force of the waves.

The local council were dragging their feet on the matter and Mirabel wrote a letter on March 29th 1977 – a month when storms raged unabated and the sea at times topped the wall – to the chief executive officer of Medina Borough Council at Newport, quoting the £40,000 estimate for a proposed repair scheme she had received from the Westridge Construction company.

Since this sea erosion is now rapidly doing serious damage we would request that your Council finance this scheme (with the necessary Government assistance), to which we – speaking on behalf of the people in this locality

– would be prepared to make a 25% contribution. As time is of major importance we look forward to your reply and trust we may hope for your early and sympathetic consideration.

The job was finally completed to everyone's satisfaction but this was just one of many clashes Mirabel had with the local authority.

The committee of the Seaview Regatta were very grateful for her unfailing support over the years with a generous annual donation of £50. In addition, Jim and Pat sent their annual donation of £15 each. Stratford St John, president of the Seaview Regatta, included in his letter of profuse thanks an invitation; 'My wife and I are giving an after-the Regatta drinks party at the Masonic Hall at 6.30 on Tuesday, 24th August and we would be so glad if you can come. We will look forward to meeting you.'

Although willing to help with financial support and a liberal offering of her business acumen, Mirabel avoided mixing socially with those whom she had only a casual acquaintance. She rarely attended cocktail parties and similar gatherings, disliking the small talk with people with whom she had nothing in common. Quite apart from the fact that at that time she could not stand for very long, she considered her sojourn on the island her special time in which to relax and unwind, a break from the necessary socialising which she obligatory carried out as mistress of Aintree. She sent a letter to Stratford St John expressing her thanks and regrets that friends were staying and therefore she was booked up.

A letter from Brigadier RN Ohlenschlager in July 1978, president of the Seaview Regatta, thanked her for her most generous donation, adding, 'With costs rising at an alarming rate our annual battle to make ends meet becomes more close fought every year and it is only because of our loyal supporters such as yourself we win in the end.' Mirabel commented that it was a letter obviously penned by an Army man.

In 1977, she covered the cost of reinstalling a diving board in the bay for public use. She was thanked by the president who, anxious not to diminish the value of her kind gesture, explained that the diving board had arrived too late for the committee to change their present programme held from the Yacht Club staging which was a popular event enjoyed by many spectators.

This combined both the pole and diving events in the same place and it was impossible at such a late stage to split the two. He continued, 'I do hope you understand the difficulty and no doubt next year the fact that there is a diving board in the bay will play a very large part in deciding the venue for the event. In the meantime I know that with the existence of the diving board the swimming events will be much easier to hold.'

Mirabel replied,

Thank you for your letter. I quite understand. A committee must be businesslike and arrange everything well in advance and even then I expect you have headaches. I feel sure the diving board will be appreciated both for pleasure and practice, although the council was not in favour of giving us permission! I will take it in and put it out each season which should keep it in good order. It is good to see the weather looks like being nice and we wish you a very enjoyable success with the regatta.

Her elegant London home was a Nash house at 18 Hanover Terrace, Regent's Park, where she employed a cook, who lived in the basement, and when Mirabel was in residence she hired a butler and maid to help entertain in style celebrities, racing personalities and the aristocracy. She was the longest standing Crown tenant in Regent's Park.

Before each visit Mirabel wrote the cook her instructions:

March 15th 1958, Dear Cook: I do not know what arrangements you are making for Easter but we shall be arriving on the night of Saturday the 5th April. We are bringing down beef and horseradish sauce and cheese. Could you get in flour and eggs (as we shall want a Yorkshire pudding) onions, cabbage, potatoes, lard and mincemeat (as we would like mince pies), Robertson is a good make. Lemons for a lemon pie. Also the usual pork pie from Selfridges and packets of Jacobs crackers and Carrs Water biscuits and 1lb of coffee. We would like a coffee sponge so can you get a bottle of Camp coffee and 2 lbs of icing sugar. If you are not smothered in cash, I think you can get most of the items from Selfridges – I believe you have signed there before. In great haste and looking forward to seeing you. Yours truly.

We shall be in on the Sunday when I am expecting Mr Hillier to lunch, but we leave early on Monday for Goodwood and do not expect to get back until very late hours. If you have arranged to go out on the Sunday do not let it interfere with your arrangements as I know we can manage, but of course will welcome you if you are not otherwise engaged. Trusting all goes well with you and looking forward to seeing you. All our best wishes, yours truly.

The cook was an important asset to her London home and instructions were always written with politeness and consideration!

She enjoyed all her homes, but Paddock Lodge was her favourite. It was her command headquarters and she would move there in late autumn to celebrate Christmas and prepare with meticulous planning for the famous steeplechase as worldwide interest, in a frenzy of anticipation, focused on Aintree with the approach of March.

In the weeks preceding Grand National day, Paddock Lodge buzzed with the business activity of every aspect of the three-day meeting. All the rooms were occupied by essential staff and overnight guests were discouraged. Anyone who wrote in hopeful anticipation of somewhere to sleep during the meeting was told very firmly to book in at a hotel. If especially in favour, one might be offered the use of a camp bed.

Her battles were numerous and with her brilliant business acumen she could be a formidable opponent no matter how powerful the opposition.

At Paddock Lodge, Mirabel had a buzzer in each room and worked on a code of her own making – two buzzes for her secretary, three for her niece Pat, four for her nephew Jim and five to bring her husband. If her niece was out of hearing, Becher, her Jack Russell, would find Pat and bring her in. They were all trained to perfection.

Even when she was over 70, Mirabel often put in an eight-hour plus day. Awakening at 6 a.m., with a telephone on each side of her bed and surrounded by a mountain of files and papers she would work throughout the day. She told me: 'I am managing director, office boy, what have you. I'm like the old woman who lives in the shoe. When trouble threatens, I am the one who irons out the wrinkles.'

She was competent in so many areas. Her hobby was bee-keeping and it was not unusual for the Grand National winner to be presented with a jar of Aintree honey.

When a swarm of bees landed on garden bushes and several people in the area were stung, the police appealed to Mirabel's expertise in rounding them up. In her calf-length tweed suit, head shrouded in protective covering, she completed her mission from first bee to last and with them under her control boarded a tramcar – for home – first informing a nervous constable and petrified tram-driver that 'bees do not like people with sweaty hands and they disembowel themselves after stinging'.

Ronald was never an easy husband with whom to cope. To a lesser mortal the threatening sight of an out-of-control Ronald, in a drunken frenzy, smashing the dining room window with a walking stick, shattering precious ornaments against the wall, before turning to vent his temper on her, would have terrified most women. Not Mirabel, with the combined force of her ample figure and combat skills she would reduce him to a crumpled heap – particularly so when he kicked her beloved Scottie bitch Jeanie.

Ronald was particularly fond of La Flora Blanche – a sweet white wine – and would swill down three bottles in record time with the usual unpleasant results. Mirabel made sure the liquor cabinet was always kept locked and the case of La Flora Blanche hidden away in the cellar.

On occasions he would still find the opportunity to over-imbibe. Jim told me an amusing story about his Uncle's behaviour at a dinner party arranged by his wife. They were halfway through the pudding course when Uncle Ronald suddenly slid down to disappear under the table. Mirabel ignored the happening and turning to her niece with a bright smile remarked: 'Pat dear, I told you that you are far too liberal with the sherry in the trifle.'

Taking their lead from their hostess, the guests continued with the conversation, finished the pudding course and went on to sample the cheese and celery. They then adjourned to the drawing room for coffee, leaving Ronald in a state of oblivion under the dining table. Apart from an occasional glass of champagne, Mirabel rarely drank alcohol.

Sometimes Ronald would try to annoy and provoke her while she was working on important racecourse papers, by switching off the light. She would retaliate by mocking him with a few humiliating sharp words: 'Ronald, I feel so sorry for you. You have my greatest sympathy. You are a truly pathetic and weak figure.' This would irritate him even more for he was well aware of his lack of moral strength.

He was often the butt for her scorn. In the late 1920s when their Riley car failed to negotiate a hill, Mirabel got out to push at the rear while Ronald remained in the driving seat. They finally made it to the top but when Ronald lifted the bonnet he found the manifold glowing red with heat. He urinated on it to cool it down and they were able to carry on with their journey, Mirabel remarking: 'Ronald, that is one of the few enterprising things you have ever done!'

When they were at Aintree, his favourite hostelry was the Sefton Arms, a short distance from the racecourse. He would go out for a tipple before dinner becoming oblivious to time as the hours passed by. There were a number of occasions when their four-legged friends enjoyed his dinner or it was thrown away by his furious wife.

For Mirabel, Ronald's most distressing habit when in London, was to disappear into the night without explanation. As a former actress, she was an expert in disguise, transforming her persona when the role required. Enveloped in a black cloak and headscarf she once tailed Ronald at a distance one night to find him happily chatting up a woman of doubtful repute. Furious, she emerged from a swirl of black cape and a startled Ronald experienced the full fury of her wrath as she swung her handbag with all the force she could muster across his face and ordered him home.

On another occasion when they lived in Warwick, she again had grounds for suspicion and decided to pursue Ronald on another of his evening prowls.

She found his car parked outside a south Warwick inn and entered without ceremony to find him in a compromising situation with a companion. With the stratagem of a skilful nightclub bouncer, she dragged him outside while his friend made a swift exit into the night. For Mirabel, this was nearly the straw that broke the camel's back and she threatened to leave him.

Her nephew James Bidwell-Topham told me; 'Uncle Ronald was in tears and wept profusely, begging her to stay, promising that he would try and mend his ways and pleading that he could not live without her. Aunt eventually agreed to stay, insisting Uncle Ronald sleep in his dressing room, and my sister Pat moved into Aunt's bedroom.'

Ronald's friends were also concerned about his behaviour and lack of consideration for his wife. Early on in the marriage, a male friend wrote to him: 'For heaven's sake man buck up your ideas. You have only just married!'

Later, he would realise that to both the outside world and himself Mirabel was a formidable force without whom he could not manage. Quite apart from being noted for plain speaking, her sex was, until the late 1960s unrecognised by the Jockey Club and National Hunt Committee who had the power to grant a licence. She became a fighter in a man's world – a sphere in which she could easily have been swept aside in a tidal wave of male domination, had she not possessed the strength and courage to fight it. This quality in her marriage to Ronald Topham was her ace.

He gave her a brooch in the shape of a bee and called it the 'Queen Bee' brooch. She wore it on her lapel more or less all the time. It acknowledged in a way his capitulation to her supreme authority. It was not an easy marriage for the 'Queen Bee' of Aintree. Over the years Ronald reformed to some extent under her control but his behaviour at time was still questionable and he never got over his excessive indulgence of alcohol.

At the age of 70, described as AR Topham, 'retired of Hanover Terrace, Regent's Park', he was charged before Mr Paul Bennett, VC at Marlborough Street Magistrates Court with 'wilfully exposing himself with intent to insult any female at the rear of the Meeting Ground, Marble Arch, on 11th April 1955'.

On the previous day, Easter Monday, after an embarrassing couple of hours at Hyde Park Police Station, Ronald had been formally cautioned, charged and ordered to appear in court the next day.

Mirabel, who had been away during the day of the offence, returned to find an envelope on the hall table. On it Ronald had written 'Mrs – If I am asleep wake me up'. Inside the envelope he had written his version of the day's happenings. Mirabel was furious but swung into action, not so much for Ronald but to prevent the possible besmirching of the Topham name. She contacted her solicitor, who appointed a barrister to defend him, and she arranged for Ronald's doctor to travel from Liverpool to give evidence of a medical problem which could be quoted in Ronald's defence as a contributory factor of his behaviour.

At his first court appearance, Ronald denied the charge and was remanded on bail for seven days until April 19th when he was represented by the barrister his wife had appointed to defend him.

Police Constable Ronald Cogill told the court that he was off duty in plain clothes in Hyde Park at about 5 p.m. when he saw the prisoner sitting on the grass, wearing a raincoat which was open. His legs were crossed near the ankles and he was holding a hat in between his legs with his left hand. His right hand was underneath the hat and he appeared to be masturbating himself.

A young woman approached and as she almost reached him he said, 'Excuse me!' she looked down at him and he moved the hat away exposing his penis. The woman ran away.

Ronald's doctor, Dr Michael Garry, told the court of Ronald's history of cystitis – inflammation of the bladder – and the need to empty his bladder every hour. He had seen Mr Topham actually holding his hand on his bladder for ten to fifteen minutes to help stave off the actual passing of water.

Ronald was convicted of the offence, given an absolute discharge – used where the court, having found the offender guilty of the offence charged considers that no further action is required on its part beyond the finding of guilt – and ordered to pay 25 guineas prosecution costs. The magistrate told him: 'I haven't the slightest hesitation about convicting you. I am quite satisfied that the constable's description of what you were doing is accurate and that you attracted this young woman's attention for your own reason and then removed your hat.'

Fortunately for Ronald, a strike of 700 maintenance men in the newspaper offices closed down all of the national daily and evening newspapers printed in London between March 25th and April 20th 1955. Big news events the Fleet Street papers missed included Sir Winston Churchill's resignation, the budget, the announcement of a general election – and the misdemeanour of Ronald Topham at the rear of the meeting ground at Marble Arch. The story never reached Liverpool!

Mirabel's Roman Catholic religion was very important to her. She prayed daily for guidance and frequently appealed to the Ecclesiastical establishment to say Masses on her behalf to give her strength and guide her in the right direction. She had many friends among the clergy and their prayers helped to sustain her throughout her married life as well as in the business of running Aintree racecourse. It was a side of the 'Queen Bee' that went largely unnoticed.

Although she radiated total self-reliance and gave the impression of always being in total control, she needed the input of her faith and prayers to give her strength. Without it one wonders if her character might have been less confident but with the need to succeed instilled in her from childhood she would no doubt have soldiered on.

Catholicism filled a want of which Mirabel was obviously in need. It is interesting to note – according to Jim – that his Aunt was actually a Catholic convert. This would fit in with the fact that when her mother Nellie Hillier died on 11th March 1943 at the age of 74 she had a Church of England funeral service.

On December 15th 1915 – a year before her engagement to Ronald – Father W Bernard Dyer, Priest at St Francis Church, Pottery Lane, Notting Hill, wrote to Mirabel:

Dear Miss Hillier
Thank you for your two notes. I am sorry that they are working you to death. Let me know when days of freedom dawn again for you, and I shall be very pleased to have the pleasure of resuming our talks on matters doctrinal and

various. I wish you a happy New Year and that it will be
filled with Blessings. Believe me,
Yours sincerely,
W Bernard Dyer.

Over the years to follow, Father Dyer became her mentor and one of her closest friends, with encouragement, prayers and guidance when Ronald sorely tried her patience. He officiated at their wedding ceremony in 1922. There is no doubt that Father Dyer's direction in steering her along the devotional path of Catholicism helped to fill an essential part of her life as the 'Queen Bee' of Aintree. Until the day she died she was faithful to the Church – always thankful for their help along the way of her travails.

The Tophams were a devout Roman Catholic family. Mirabel went on a pilgrimage to Lourdes early in her marriage and Ronald, like his wife, followed the doctrines of the Church faithfully – if straying a little off course on the way! Early in their engagement, Father Dyer had come to her rescue in dealing with Ronald's hurtful attitude towards her.

Mirabel was always generous with her gifts and donations to the church. In 1929, the Parish Priest of a church at Hampton-on-the-Hill, near Warwick, wrote:

Dear Mrs Topham – May I thank you on behalf of St Charles Congregation for the really beautiful statue of St Anthony and its pedestal. I am sure that the prayers of those who have devotion to this great Saint will be in unison with mine and that in return for your generosity St Anthony will grant you protection and every request you make for favours. With renewed thanks and every good wish from yours sincerely. Parish Priest.

Headed 'Praise be to Jesus Christ', a letter dated February 19th 1959 from the Convent of Poor Clares Collettine was sent to:

My dear Mrs Topham, Jim and Pat. GOD REWARD YOU ALL for the kind thought at Christmas, and the really magnificent box of chocolates. I do not think I've seen finer. We are sure to enjoy the contents, and think of you. We wish you every grace and blessing and prayed much for you during the Christmas holidays, and will continue to do so throughout the year.

We here had a beautiful Christmas, spiritually and otherwise, with extra recreations, and plenty of fun. Our novice is a real comedian, and very generously gave herself and her time for our amusement. Towards the end of the holidays a new postulant arrived, whom we looked upon as a very substantial Christmas Gift. She is a nice child, about 21 or 22, with much sense and fun in her – both so essential for a Poor Clare Collettine. She has a brother trying his vocation with the Capuchins, so it will be very nice if they both persevere.

Our dear Mother Clare is still with us, though going down step by step – very bravely and contentedly – we do love her. With very much love to you all – God Bless You... Many thanks, and reassurance of prayers.

Mirabel was helped personally in times of private grief and business conflict by her prayers for guidance and the support of the Church. Such a time preceded the six-day action at the Civil Court of the Liverpool Assizes when she was involved in a legal dispute over the dismissal of her clerk of the course, Douglas Montague Wood and his action for damages. It was obvious that for this occasion

Mirabel was going to need all her wits about her and the hand of divine intervention.

A letter from the Convent of Poor Clares at Knowle, Warwickshire, dated June 12th 1936 read:

My dearest Ron and Mirrie
I understand that the case is to come off on the 22nd.
It is a big ordeal for you as I hear that Peers are to give
evidence. So I send this as a cheerio. Keep up your courage
and trust in Prayer. I enclose a picture of Saint Thomas
More, take him in your pocket and we will pray hard to
the martyrs for you, they have done many things for this
community. On the Day, we will ask the Holy Spirit to
help and inspire you with the right and best things to
say. Don't worry. (To Ronald) I cant imagine you in the
witness box, poor old thing, you and Mirrie will have to
be very calm and dignified! Don't try to get a lot out, but
answer straight to the point. I am terribly sorry for you to
have to go through it all. May God grant all will be well,
of course, I shall be longing for news.
We must not forget to invoke St Joseph, St Benedict and
St Anthony who have always taken care of Aintree. Well
goodbye old chap for today.
With very much love to you both and may God bless you
and be with you always…
Ever your loving old sister in Jesus Christ…
M Angela of Divine Love.

A second letter from the Convent of Poor Clares posted four days later read:

My dearest Ron and Mirrie: So glad to get your card.
Glad that the case starts on Friday the Feast of the Sacred
Heart … I am sure you will be having Masses offered

on the days. I will ask our Abbess to promise one here in thanksgiving if all goes well. She is very anxious for you to promise something if you win, in honour of St John Fisher and St Thomas More. The Archbishop and Bishop are most anxious to get devotion to them propagated and I can assure we did have a real miracle last year through their intercession, if not more than one, and we don't mean them to let us down now! Take courage and do manfully and keep up your spirits all through. Though things may look black at first, some little thing may come along to turn the tide. Indeed if God is with you, what matter how great the odds against you.

Poor old Mirrie, you are a brick, never mind the bad bits, in any case no true gentleman would ever bring a lady before the Court. Of course we shall be at our Prayers. I am sure if we all trust in Prayer, when the time comes, you will both have the grace of the moment, to do the right thing and go through calmly and bravely. Ron can recall facing the enemy in a dugout or a trench and like Nelson he can turn his blind eye to the crowd. Keep Saint Thomas More's twinkle in your eye! He was splendid and never would take a case or go on with one, if he found it was unjust, no matter how much he might lose.

God bless you both and help you. A deeper thought still is Christ's own trial that will give you the greatest calmness and strength. You will be constantly in our thoughts and prayers. The Abbess sends her love. Your loving old sister in Christ…

M. Angela of the Divine Love.

During her reign as chairman and managing director of Aintree, trouble threatened on many occasions and her battles made headlines. This court action was the most sensational. It took place within two years of her becoming a director in 1935 and was widely reported as the 'Aintree Racecourse Lawsuit' in the Liverpool and national press.

Two of the star witnesses were Lord Derby, a steward at Aintree, and the Earl of Sefton, senior steward of Aintree, a member of the Jockey Club and the National Hunt Committee.

The outcome was not as she had hoped. Mr Justice Lewis gave judgement in favour of Mr Wood, the company was ordered to pay him £3,250 damages plus the costs of the case amounting to nearly £6,000 and there were harsh words for Mirabel.

The case proved a revelation of the workings of Tophams Ltd, under the influence of Mirabel, their recently appointed board member, who was described in Court as their 'Ring Leader'. The story, which emerged, captivated the racing fraternity and members of the public. It revealed yet another dimension of Mirabel's remarkable strength of character, ability and ambition to control.

The case was one in which Douglas Montague Wood, aged 50, former deputy managing director of Tophams Ltd, claimed damages for wrongful dismissal or breach of contract. Both sides were represented by the elite of the legal hierarchy – Tophams by DF Maxwell Fyfe, KC MP and HI Nelson. Wood was represented by Norman Birkett KC and FE Pritchard.

Mirabel swept into the court entrance each morning to the popping of cameras photographing her in a variety of elegant outfits and hats chosen to suit the occasion, and with the aplomb of an actress in the star role.

She had received a letter of encouragement from her mother the day before the case.

She wrote:

My dear Mirrie

*Just a line to wish you the very best of luck on Friday
and the following days. Don't forget Friday is your Lucky
Day. Wear something that you feel happy in and be your
own natural self and you'll be alright.*

Fond Love

Mother.

Wood claimed that a written agreement of December
19, 1933 appointing him deputy managing director of the
company, and clerk of the racecourse for a seven-year
period from January 1 1934 was still in force, and that he
was entitled to receive his salary (£1,200), fees (£200), and
expenses (£100) for this period. He claimed an injunction
to restrain Tophams from appointing during that time
any other person to that position. Alternatively he asked
for damages for breach of agreement and wrongful
dismissal.

The defence was that it was a term of the agreement that
Wood carry out the instructions of the managing director
or board of directors which he had not done and that
he had failed in his duty to advise the board on matters
connected with racing. Wood said he had committed no
misconduct or failed to carry out his duties.

Birkett alleged that the Tophams had secretly plotted
to get Wood out of the company, 'because it is clear from
correspondence the real trouble is that Wood is not a
Topham.

'All was harmony until Mrs Topham joined the board.
I don't hesitate to say, on the evidence before me, that Mrs
Topham is the chief cause of all this trouble. She must be
a very remarkable woman. Certainly it is plain from the
evidence that she dominates her husband.'

Mr Justice Lewis: 'This action is not framed on conspiracy, but for breach of contract and wrongful dismissal.'

Mr Birkett agreed but the matters on which the company relied were 'trivial and trumpery'.

Referring to the question of damages, Mr Birkett added that the judge would appreciate the position of a clerk of the course was a peculiar one. Mr Wood had been working in that capacity since the war, and was unable to get another position comparable to it.

In evidence, Wood said he had known various members of the Topham family since 1908 and had a friendship with William (WW) Topham (EAC Topham's younger brother who was appointed a director in 1911) for 31 years. In 1919 he was invited by them to join the company and was subsequently elected a director and secretary. He now held 63 shares valued at £6,300. He assisted Mr EAC Topham, clerk of the course, until Mr Topham died in 1932. By that time he had familiarised himself with the duties of a clerk of the course and was appointed to succeed EAC Topham.

During 1934, his first year under agreement, there had been no trouble. In that year a resolution giving clerk of the course responsibility for official and complimentary badges, became a source of great annoyance when Mrs Topham joined the board and she objected strongly.

Wood: 'My view was that complimentary badges, other than those acquired by members of the board, should be dealt with by me.'

Fyfe: 'Was your attitude in 1935, I am clerk of the course. I am responsible for complimentary badges. I am not going to have interference from management?'

Wood: 'No, there was no question of interference. They gave me complimentary badges, and I dealt with them, and if they wanted any they instructed me.'

There was further trouble about some commissions received, as agent, on the insurance of, among other things, fences at the course and office furniture. Members of the board wanted commissions to go, in future, to the company.

The form of the racecard was another issue of contest. Mirabel wanted Wood's name removed from the card and the name of Topham to have greater prominence. There had been other changes in presentation with which she did not agree. 'The Management reserve the right to refuse admission', had been replaced without consultation to 'The Stewards reserve the right to refuse admission'.

Wood sought the advice of the stewards of the Jockey Club, and as a result Lord Derby attended a full meeting of the board, at which he told members that under rule 22 of the Rules of Racing, the clerk of the course was solely responsible to the stewards for the arrangements for the meetings and official racecards. The clerk of the course was the servant of the stewards and authorised by them, and nobody could take his place. Wood's name should appear on the card.

The Jockey Club had decided that the only person who could put notices in the racing calendar was the clerk of the course and the Tophams had no right to dictate to the clerk of the course what should be put in. The company had nothing whatever to do with the notices. The relationship between the directors and the clerk of the course had nothing to do with the stewards.

All they were out to see was that the Laws of Racing were strictly carried out. The company was perfectly entitled to make representation to the stewards if they were not satisfied with Wood's conduct, but they would have to prove that he had done something contrary to the Rules of Racing. Lord Derby also pointed out that the authority of the stewards must be secured before anyone was appointed in his place. 'It would require a great deal to shake the confidence in Mr Wood, who, in my opinion, from a sporting point of view, is a most admirable clerk of the course.'

Lord Derby continued: 'I went to the meeting because, to use a colloquialism, I am thoroughly fed up with all the arguing between Mr Wood and them. I thought if I could knock their heads together, it might be possible to get some agreement.'

Birkett: 'Were your views acceptable to the directors?'

Lord Derby: 'There was only one director who spoke, and that was Mrs Topham.'

Birkett: 'Did Mrs Topham appear pleased with your views?'

Lord Derby: 'Oh no, she didn't agree with my views and I am sorry to say I got rather impatient.'

Birkett: 'Did Mrs Topham seek to contradict the view you had laid down as to the attitude of the stewards to the clerk of the course?'

Lord Derby: 'I think she had only one idea in mind, and that was to do something against Mr Wood. With regard to his duties as clerk of the course, I did not hear her say one word. She asked that the name of Tophams should continue to appear on the cards.

'There was a vast difference between the position when EAC Topham was clerk of the course and the present directorate. There was nothing EAC did not know about racing.

'I have not the same opinion about the present directorate with regard to their knowledge of racing. I am perfectly certain that the general racing public would agree. Old Topham knew it all but the present directors know nothing about it.'

During the meeting, Lord Derby had taken exception to Mirabel Topham's observations and rebuked her. He later wrote her a letter of apology and explained that 'my rebuke was made in the heat of the moment'.

Lord Sefton told the court, 'he was in complete agreement with Lord Derby, and had had an interview with the Topham directors and Mr Wood, at Aintree racecourse during one of the race meetings'.

He said 'As senior steward, I called them together and told them I don't want any discussion. I want to put before you the view of the stewards regarding the clerk of the course. You can take it or leave it. We must go and watch the next race.'

Wood alleged that at a meeting with Mrs Topham she said that he had not put into the racecard what they wanted him to do. She regretted the absence from the racecard of the name Topham, so long associated with it. 'You have broken your contract,' she said 'and this is what we wanted you to do.' She objected to his giving his office address as The Adelphi Hotel and not Aintree racecourse.

Mr Justice Lewis said the company were entitled to decide where his office should be. Wood agreed, explaining that what went into the racing calendar was between the company, the clerk of the course and the Jockey Club, who could within reason prevent anything from going into the calendar they did not want. It would have been the concern of the Jockey Club if anything had happened at the meeting and the address was the wrong place. His idea was to prevent this happening. People might send telegrams regarding colours, declarations or letter which might easily go astray.

Cross-examined by Fyfe, Wood admitted that the day before the funeral of EAC Topham, a resolution was passed by a meeting of two directors that he should take over the duties as clerk of the course and application was made to the stewards immediately for him to be appointed, before the board had been brought up to the minimum of three directors.

Fyfe: 'That was the fountain origin of the trouble, that you had been appointed by yourself and Mr Willie Topham, before members of the company had any chance to consider it?'

Wood: 'Yes.'

Fyfe: 'During the early part of 1933 the objection of the members of the family was that you were then managing director, clerk of the course and secretary.'

Wood: 'Quite.'

Fyfe: 'And they wanted the board reconstituted so that there should be more Topham about it?'

Birkett: 'Mr Topham, one of the directors, married a lady, an actress, who had no knowledge of racing whom counsel did not hesitate to say on the evidence before him at any rate was the chief cause of all the trouble. I allege that Mr and Mrs Topham and Mr Hedley – another director – were secretly plotting so that they could get Mr Wood out of the company. It was clear from the correspondence the real trouble was that Wood was not a Topham. Up to the moment when the requisitions were put in that every director must be a member of the Topham family, there could be no question of mismanagement by Wood at all.'

Giving evidence, Mirabel Topham said that during 1934 she was not satisfied with the way the company was being run. Wood had not been complying with his contract, neither with the terms nor the spirit. The directors had objected to alterations Wood made in the racing card and desired that Messrs Tophams should sign the card as a firm.

She alleged that Wood was 'trying to get control of

Tophams, and was not behaving like a loyal friend of the company. I agree he in no way upset the stewards but I do not agree he was an excellent clerk, because he did not come to the board and give us the support he should.'

Birkett: 'Let us face the issue. You were arming yourself to attack the clerk of the course the moment you went on the board?'

Mrs Topham: 'Yes, I agree if you put it that way.'

Birkett: 'You came on the board as a result of a well thought out scheme?'

Mrs Topham: 'No.'

Birkett: 'Wasn't it arranged between you and Mr Hedley before you came on the board, that you would put him in the chair and dispose of Mr William Topham?'

Mrs Topham: 'Yes.'

Birkett: 'That you should get rid of Mr Dent, the secretary?'

Mrs Topham: 'Yes.'

Birkett: 'And that you should endeavour to curtail the activities of Mr Wood inasmuch as to keep the management in control?'

Mrs Topham: 'Yes, but not to interfere with the clerk of the course.'

Birkett: 'For you to do this you were to go on the board?'

Mrs Topham: 'Yes.'

Birkett: 'And for you to go on the board, I suggest, Mr Mark Topham was disposed in your favour?'

Mrs Topham: 'Yes.'

Ronald Topham was called to give evidence.

Birkett: 'You have heard your wife say that she was the dominating mind in your marriage?'

Topham: 'Well most men are influenced by their wives. I use my own common sense in some matters.'

Birkett: 'But you rather like the easy life don't you',

recalling that Mrs Topham described the men of the family as 'shy, retiring and nervous'?

Topham: 'Yes.'

Birkett: 'Did you take part in 1934 in discussions between your wife and Mr Hedley.'

Topham: 'At some part I used to fall asleep.'

Birkett: 'At what part of the meeting did you fall asleep?'

Topham: 'At the beginning. It was a weakness of nature.'

Birkett: 'I suppose you felt comfortable, knowing your wife would carry it through?'

Topham: 'Well I felt great confidence in her abilities.'

Birkett: 'It wasn't much use saying anything if you wanted to?'

Topham: 'I don't agree with that.'

Birkett: 'When you awakened you would say "OK"? It was a favourite expression of yours?'

Granting judgement in favour of Wood, Mr Justice Lewis referred to Mirabel Topham as the ringleader in the policy pursued by the board with regard to Wood and said that she completely dominated her husband. Referring to Ronald Topham, the Judge said that he took very little interest in the company, and he might say at that stage he had formed the opinion that WW Topham and AR Topham were 'complete nonentities'.

They had little or no knowledge of racing, and, in fact, were content to let things slide, with the result that in 1933 Wood, a great friend of WW Topham, got the complete upper hand and, in fact, ran Mr WW Topham and was really in control of the board.

That conduct undoubtedly led certain members of the Topham family to set themselves the task of getting control of the management of the company out of the hands of

Wood. The ringleader was Mrs AR Topham, a person of dominating and masterful character and personality and no doubt of considerable business acumen. Not only did she dominate everyone with whom she came in contact, but she completely dominated her husband.

The evidence he gave showed this, and it was not going too far to say that he frankly admitted that his wife controlled him. It was certain that when EAC Topham died certain members of the family were anxious that control should not pass out of the Topham family.

The Judge referred to a letter of February 20th, 1933, sent to AR Topham by GW Hedley, a retired schoolmaster and director. It was obvious that there might have been more than one previous communication, because the letter spoke of 'clipping the wings' of Wood.

The Judge was satisfied that Hedley, who owing to illness had not been able to give evidence, had been approached by AR Topham, or more probably Mrs Topham, with a view to his joining the campaign against Wood. Hedley's knowledge of company matters could only be equalled to his ignorance of racing matters, and he was totally unsuited to assume, as he did eventually, the chairmanship of the company.

After the court cleared, Mirabel, skilfully, and with good humour, talked with the throng of reporters and photographers waiting outside. Then, taking her husband's arm, she propelled him to their car, urging: 'Do get a move on Ronald, it's more than time for a cup of tea.'

During her reign as chairman and managing director of Aintree the Grand National gained enormous popularity. The newsreel companies accepted it and films of the great race were shown on cinema screens throughout the world. She fought the BBC over commentary rights, refusing to let them broadcast it and organised her own lacklustre commentary, which proved to be one of her few failures.

Eventually the BBC were forced to acknowledge Tophams' copyright. Lack of television revenue took its toll on profits and in 1960 finally, she decided it was prudent to sign a deal with the BBC to televise the race. The first radio commentary conducted by the BBC was in 1927.

Dealing with Mirabel had not been an easy job for Peter Dimmock, head of BBC Television Outside Broadcasts. He had successfully negotiated, with no problems, for TV broadcasts from Sandown Park, Kempton and Royal Ascot. Formidable Mirabel was a more difficult act and throughout the fifties proved a tough negotiator before finally consenting, and the Grand National became the greatest annual television event of that time.

There were no hard feelings between Peter Dimmock and Mirabel. He became her friend and with his wife, television celebrity Polly Elwes, enjoyed her generous hospitality on Grand National day. He told me: 'Mirabel was indeed an exceptional person – a velvet glove often hid a tough exterior.'

Mirabel was godmother to their daughter Amanda, a popular role for she had no children of her own. Amanda was a bright, pretty little girl amusing to be with and had inherited much of the charm and personality of her mother.

Amanda possessed many of the entertaining characteristics so admired by Mirabel and in addition had an affinity with the theatre by way of her mother who had trained at the Central School of Drama and acted on stage at Windsor and London theatres before embarking on a career in television.

Mirabel fulfilled admirably her obligations to all her godchildren and Amanda remembers her with love and appreciation for the care and interest 'Aunty Tops' devoted to the responsibility of being her godmother.

When Mirabel died in 1980, Pat and Jim, who were very fond of Amanda, willingly accepted the continuance of their Aunt's role with visits, lunches, dinners and long telephone calls.

They had accompanied Mirabel when she attended Amanda's christening at the Kensington Catholic Church in 1961. Mirabel's present for the baby, a silver porringer engraved with small animals and accompanied by a card reading 'From her Godmother 1961' is much treasured. Amanda's birthday on 7th August is the day after Mirabel's.

Even so it was unlikely that 'Aunty Tops' would ever have forgotten her goddaughter's special day. Much to the delight of her young friends, a large lady in a flowing gown and gorgeous hat would emerge with a beaming smile from her Rolls Royce with arms full of presents.

Usually accompanied by Jim and Pat, she greeted all the children affectionately and sampled the birthday tea. The children watched in delighted anticipation for the birthday girl to open the array of prettily packed gifts.

On occasions, her presents reflected Mirabel's own philosophy of life and contained a message that could be inspirational to Amanda on her journey through life.

This was evident in her gift of a poem written by Mirabel and framed on the back of a print of *Lottery* ridden by J Mason and owned by J Elmore the first winner of the Grand National Steeplechase in 1839.

The Grand National Steeplechase
By Mirabel Topham

You ask me to name my favourite Gee
That ran in this great Chase's history

I lay no claim to select the Great
Or argue on Pace, or carrying Weight.
The charm of this Chase is its so like Life
Needing Courage, Skill and how to dodge strife
For Dame Fortune opens her arms here wider
To give full chance to a game outsider.

I'll give you Lottery. *It's a great name.*
It heads Aintree's list of horses of Fame.
It is also something waiting for you.
A true Tester in life as you go through.

Never be cocksure you're going to win
Too much presumptions considered a sin
Just when you think you had climbed to the top
Something may give and you'll come down a flop.

Whatever you aim at – go in with Zest
And make sure always to give of your best
Then if you should lose just lose with a smile
Counting the effort an effort worthwhile.

From your Godmother
MDT

Another present to Amanda with a particularly significant Aintree/Mirabel connection was a brooch in an oval of ivory with a silver racehorse and mounted jockey on top and a silver scalloped surround.

It came with a letter from Jim:

Dear Amanda
I thought you would like to know the history of the lovely
brooch you have received today on Auntie's behalf.

66

In 1949 our Company, Tophams Limited, instituted a new steeplechase at Aintree to be called the Topham Trophy, and it was the subject of an annual art competition to be held at the Walker Art Gallery in Liverpool.

The winner of the first competition was an artist named A K Wiffen and he later made this Ivory and Silver Brooch and presented it to Auntie as a special gift.

She was delighted and it became one of her favourite brooches.

Lots of love from Jimmy

Mirabel hoped that Amanda would follow her own love of music and bought her a clarinet. She tried it for a while but eventually gave up in favour of the piano.

As a child she visited the Tophams on the Isle of Wight for a week every year. Her father, who had joined the BBC in 1946 after his demob from the RAF when he had been first a pilot and then an Air Ministry Staff Officer, would fly her down. On other occasions Jim would drive her there. These treats were very special for a youngster and she recalls, 'I was the envy of my sisters who were never invited and my holidays with the Tophams were the highlight of my year.

'At about this time Aunty Tops was eighty and weighed about eighteen stones. She spent most days in her bedroom in a huge double bed with racecourse papers scattered all over the coverlet. I would visit her in the bedroom for a brief chat and always was greeted with affection. I did not see a great deal of her and it was Pat and Jimmy who kept me entertained and looked after me very well. They were wonderful and knew just how to keep a child happy and occupied. Pat was a fantastic cook and we had super food. We toured the island, had a trip in the hovercraft, played ball on the beach with the dog, and I swam with Pat. In the evenings we played Monopoly and other games and Jimmy told ghost stories. It was all tremendous fun.

'When I was about twelve the invitations to holiday with them on the island suddenly ended. I was puzzled and worried in case I had offended them in any way. All was revealed by a relative of Mirabel who told me that the rule applied to all of Mirabel's godchildren and young visitors. Before the age of twelve children were so easy to entertain and amuse but as teenagers the Topham trio did not know what to do with them!'

Although the Isle of Wight holidays finished when Amanda became a teenager she was always part of the Tophams extended family. Mirabel, Pat and Jim attended her first Communion and collected her in their large black Rolls Royce for the drive to and from church. She was often a guest on Grand National day.

When Mirabel's health deteriorated she still telephoned and after the deaths of both Mirabel and Pat, Jim continued to fulfil the role Aunty Tops had vacated, treating Amanda to lunches and dinners. He attended her wedding in 1987 and remained close to the family until his death. John and Ruaidhri, Amanda's children, greatly enjoyed Uncle Jimmy's abundant supply of ghost stories and starry-eyed pleaded for more. It all gave credence to the fact that children were much easier to entertain than teenagers.

Mirabel had much to do with the introduction of the Levy Board in the early 1960s, although at the time Aintree was one of the courses that considered it had been far from fairly treated by them. The Liverpool executive supported the retention of bookmakers and were not in favour of a Tote monopoly.

At the height of the Cold War it was her initiative that was instrumental in persuading the Soviet government that it would be a good idea to enter Russian horses in the National. It was a propaganda coup, not only for Aintree, but also for the Soviets themselves and resulted in much publicity – although on race day there were no winning results for the Russian horses.

Mirabel was a brilliant communicator and possessed the skill to negotiate at speed and effectively with a wide range of individuals and groups – stable lads, trainers, accountants and bookmakers. She was a no-nonsense woman, demanding a square deal for the racecourse, and had no time for fools or opportunists. She battled with the racing news agencies by raising the rental of on-course telephones.

In 1949 Tophams Ltd, purchased the racecourse from the Earl of Sefton, the freehold costing £275,000. A forward thinker, Mirabel masterminded the construction of the Mildmay course built within the established National course and named after Lord Mildmay, a superb amateur jockey and Grand National enthusiast. The Mildmay course opened in 1953, and in the following year, another of her innovations, in a bid to generate new income, was the motor circuit which encircled the track.

Mirabel's ambitious planning did not have an easy ride. Controversy raged and there were lengthy discussions with the various parties affected. One of the biggest obstacles was the re-routing of a public footpath on the course. A public inquiry followed and finally in 1954 she obtained a licence to stage a motor race.

Assisted by the Duke of Richmond and Gordon – who owned Goodwood – Mirabel brought international motor racing to Merseyside by contracting for the laying of a three miles Grand Prix circuit, where in 1957 the Prix d'Europe was run. Aintree was the first purpose-built Grand Prix track in the UK. It was opened in 1954 and the first Grand Prix was run in 1955.

For 11 years, Aintree played host to the cream of British motor racing, on the circuit that ran alongside the horse racing course. From 1955 until 1964, the venue staged four British and one European Grand Prix with the best drivers in the world competing. Stirling Moss made history in 1957 by being the first British driver to win a Grand Prix in a British car, a 'Vanwall' loaned to him by his team mate Tony Brooks, when Moss's own car hit trouble.

Mercedes, Jaguar and Ferrari teams raced there, with drivers like Mike Hawthorn, Juan Fangio, Jim Clark and Graham Hill competing in an era when Britain ruled the sport.

The motor track also assisted Aintree in its television contract with the BBC, enabling millions to see the race.

Even after the big races went elsewhere, Aintree continued as a club race circuit until the 1980s using a loop to take the cars away from the main complex. A celebration was held in 2005 to commemorate the anniversary of the first Grand Prix at Aintree.

Another minor skirmish for Mirabel was with a local councillor who objected – unsuccessfully – to Tophams erecting high fences along the canal bank which locals used to get a free view of the course.

She dealt with every issue personally. A letter dated January 24th 1958 from R Fletcher of Timperley, Cheshire complained:

Dear Madam, I recently had the misfortune to visit Aintree racecourse and I would like to register a complaint about the accommodation afforded to patrons in the Cheap Ring. In the first instance I was very much surprised to find that the entrance fee was three shillings and sixpence as compared with many other racecourses where the charge is only three shillings. However, I was not perturbed over this slight increase because I felt sure that the wide publicity given to this famous racecourse and under such able management as yourself must excel in its amenities to the racing public.

Alas, Mrs Topham, you and the racecourse authorities at Liverpool have disgusted me! You certainly do not cater for the patrons of your cheap ring and yet you charge more than other courses.

The attendance in the Cheap Ring on the day I visited was very poor and no wonder! It was raining but there is nowhere to shelter – not even a decent snack bar to offer a roof whilst having a cup of tea. As for seeing the racing, I admit you could see the last jump of the steeplechase course, and also two furlongs of the run-in on the hurdle course, but only if you stood on two bricks! I tried to find a racecourse steward to register my complaints but they were as scarce as the rest of Aintree's amenities.

Don't you think, Mrs Topham, it would be in the better interests of the racing public if you were to devote more of your energy towards putting your house in order at home instead of devoting so much of your time trying to scheme thousands of pounds out of the radio and television services? I feel sure that you will present this letter at your next board meeting and I imagine the general opinion will be to Hell with him, let him keep his three shillings and sixpence, but remember also, that while I have voiced my opinion of your so-called famous racecourse; many thousands will be thinking the same as I do but they do not write.

Yours faithfully.

Mirabel replied with a personal letter:

Thank you for your letter. I am always pleased to receive constructive criticism, as it is usually helpful. I should like to deal with the points you raise in that order.

Admission charge: The financial upkeep of the Aintree racecourse with fences that are built differently to any others in this country or I believe in the world, is far in excess of other courses, and it is a headache in these days to retain this distinction.

Snack Bars and Shelter: There are several, but if the attendance is poor on a wet day, the caterers only open one or two. I will endeavour to see that this is remedied in the future.

Viewing: I just cannot think what happened to you as you can see the racing right round the course from this enclosure at the December meeting if you walk from one side to the other.

TV and Radio: Are already proving a danger to the racing sports promoters but a boom to off-the-course-bookmakers who pay nothing for the material they use. I feel convinced that you would not let anyone give your goods away without receiving a fair payment, we certainly cannot afford to do this.

Amenities: Sorry if these are not all you could wish for, but it will be many years before we see any return on the £63,000 spent on this enclosure in 1950. Of course we want you to come to the races or we should not have spent the above amount of money, but do remember the programme (jumping) that you get at Aintree you cannot get anywhere else in the world... and that just has to be paid for.

With the best of good wishes.

Another letter from a gentleman at Brighton asked:

Dear Madame. I beg that you will pardon the liberty I am taking in writing to you, but I have a small request to make. Will you generously honour me with your autograph, as an addition to my 'private' collection? I hasten to assure you of my thanks, should you favour me, and I hope you will not refuse. I beg to remain Dear Madame yours respectfully Alfred.

Mirabel was happy to oblige.

Mirabel Topham was an enthusiastic patron of the arts, and a generous benefactor of the Walker Art Gallery in Liverpool. She initiated an annual competition from 1949 for the design and manufacture of a trophy for the Topham Trophy steeplechase, a race held during the Grand National meeting, and now reinstated in the Grand National race programme.

Post-war crowds at Aintree boomed and at one time were said to number 150,000 but in 1960 they began to dwindle significantly at the hurdle and flat race meetings and the huge upkeep of Aintree was becoming onerous.

Mirabel appealed for help to keep the Grand National steeplechase in the forefront. Ireland had always been well represented at Aintree and their enthusiastic support was illustrated in their response to her appeal. Over the years 1958–1963 they contributed £30,000 from their world famous Sweepstake. It was a generous gesture but a drop in the ocean.

Ronald died suddenly in November 1958 aged 73, and in spite of many hard knocks Mirabel managed to keep the Aintree flag flying high, soldiering on as family head and boss of Aintree. Only when resources, both physical and financial, were dwindling and maintenance expenses and red tape were strangling Tophams Ltd, was it sadly decided to stage the 'finale'.

In 1964, when she was 72 – 30 years after she joined the board – she said the course she had bought from the Earl of Sefton in 1949 was to be sold for commercial development and the 1965 National would be the last.

The on-off saga of the sale of Aintree continued for another nine years until 1973 but for Mirabel Topham there was one last battle to be fought, and it was with the 'Top Brass'.

Mirabel may have been the Queen Bee but the indisputable 'Royals' of Aintree racecourse with the grandeur of rank and course connections steeped in the past, were the Earls of Sefton and Derby. Their noble lineage had been part of an illustrious syndicate consisting of the Earls of Derby, Sefton, Eglington and Wilton, Lord George Bentinck, Lord Stanley, Lord Robert Grosvenor with seven other important North Country sporting gentlemen, who combined to bring the Liverpool Chase from Maghull to Aintree in the early 1800s.

A poem of great interest to Mirabel described how the name 'steeple' chasing may have originated. She had no idea from whom or where the poem emanated but to her way of thinking it set the scene for the spectacular contests of speed and endurance, which became the Grand National steeplechase.

One day some jovial huntsmen when
Returning from the chase,
Each boasting of his horse's speed
Decided on a race,
The goal to be the village church, its
Steeple all could see,

And he that touched the building first
The winner was to be.
With tally ho! And harkaway! Across
The country straight
They rode, and cleared all in their way
The ditch – the hedge – the gate.
The sport then new, it quickly grew – it
Spread from place to place,
And folks would come from near and
Far to see a 'steeple' chase.

It could well have been inspired about the time of the first Grand National in 1839. The title and conditions of that 1839 race were as follows:

The Grand National Steeplechase – A sweepstake of 20 sovereigns each, 5 Forfeit, with 100 added; 12 stone, each gentlemen rider; 4 miles across the country, the second to save his stake, and the winner to pay 10 sovereigns towards expenses. No rider to open a gate or ride through a gateway or more than 100 yards along any road, footpath or driftway.

It was in 1839 that bearded rider Captain Becher leaped into fame by landing in a dirty brook. His ducking is commemorated to this day with one of the National course's most difficult obstacles – 'Bechers Brook' – bearing his name.

Mirabel Topham had a special interest in the story of *Voluptuary*, the horse on which EP Wilson won in 1884, which was destined to become a theatre favourite. At the end of his racing career he was engaged by the management of Drury Lane Theatre, where the sensational drama *The Prodigal Daughter* was being played to crowded houses, to appear on stage nightly ridden by actor Leonard Royne in the Grand National scene. To uproarious applause the steeplechase star jumped the water at every performance as brilliantly as he had done at Aintree.

On February 26th 1839, a clear day with heavy going, the then Earl of Sefton, acting as starter, marshalled the 17 runners taking part in the first Grand National steeplechase at Aintree – organised by the syndicate who had taken over the lease of the grandstand and racecourse.

Jem Mason's three length victory in that first National in 1839 was in a time of 14 minutes, 53 seconds. *Lottery* was a fantastic jumper and it was said at the time that he cleared ten yards over the last hurdle – a big jump at the end of a four-mile race. Incidentally Mason was an extreme dandy with an excessive amount of self-conceit. He once, in the course of a 'chase rode his horse over a new unbreakable gate, 5ft 6in high, in preference to a penetrable bullfinch hedge spread on either side of the posts. His explanation was that he intended to go to the opera that night and did not want to scratch his face!

This active and historic participation of Lords Sefton and Derby as members of the Aintree racecourse Committee from its earliest days gave them a bearing of authority which commanded deference and respect. Both Earls were stewards of the Liverpool racecourse, Lord Sefton was not only the senior steward he was also the more autocratic of the two. He was also chairman of Chester racecourse, and a steward at Newbury, Newmarket and Royal Ascot. He owned a six-seater plane, an American twin-engined Cessna, to travel to and from race meetings.

Mirabel Topham's nephew, Jim, clerk of the Aintree course for 17 years, being appointed in November 1956 and retiring in 1975 prior to the sale, told me an amusing story of when Aintree needed a new steward to fill a vacancy.

Lord Sefton presided over the meeting considering a few possible names, one of which was the soap magnate Lord Leverhulme. Lord Sefton studied the list, puffed on a large Havana cigar, and said emphatically, 'We cannot have Leverhulme; he is trade.' Lord Leverhulme did, in fact, eventually become a steward at Aintree, proving an excellent choice.

When racecourse business needed to be discussed, Jim would be summoned to the Estate Agent's office at Croxteth Hall. The Earl would stride in amid a flurry of Jack Russells – Poky, Minx and Blink. When one of his terriers had been killed on the estate roads, the Earl ordered that all the roads should have dips to stop speeding motorists. As puppies, the Jack Russells were house trained by the gamekeeper before taking residence in the hall, where water dishes were placed throughout for their convenience.

On less formal occasions, the terriers accompanied the Earl's American born wife Josephine into the dining-room and while the butler and footmen attended to her every need, Poky, Minx and Blink waited expectantly under the table for the titbits which the Countess distributed for their pleasure.

To indicate to Jim the completion of the racecourse business, the Earl nodded his head and left the Estate Agent's Office.

The Countess had a magnificent collection of jewellery, which insurance companies refused to indemnify for loss if worn while she was travelling. So she had replicas created for journeying away from Croxteth Hall and kept the real items for private parties at home.

Once, however, at one of their Grand National parties attended by the cream of the nobility, the Earl and Countess and their guests experienced an alarming security breach within the confines of the hall. After an enjoyable day of racing, wining and lunching in the comfort of the Earl's Aintree box, the guests returned to Croxteth for dinner and a game of cards before bedtime.

They were all exhausted and, instead of putting their jewellery in a place of safety, the women left it on their dressing tables before retiring. The following morning it was discovered that an intruder had entered all the bedrooms during the night and the valuable items of jewellery had been stolen while they slept. It was suspected to be an 'inside job'. The Earl instructed the police that no details of the distressing happening be made public and the result of their investigation was never revealed.

But while the Earl and others in Liverpool partied on Grand National night, the Topham trio of Mirabel, Pat and Jim preferred to sit around Jim's stoked-up log fire and reflect on the day's happenings.

The Countess was an enthusiastic supporter of Animal Welfare, and in particular the Brooke Animal Hospital in Cairo. The Hospital was founded after World War I by Major General Brooke and his wife who were appalled at the suffering of the British horses which had been shipped out from England during the conflict and left behind to be sold off as working horses in appalling conditions. Today, the work of the Brooke has expanded and is supported by many racing people. The Duchess of Cornwall and Prince Charles toured the hospital on their visit to Egypt, the Duchess having patronised the work of the Brooke Hospital for many years.

In the early days, I held a fund raising sale on it's behalf and the Countess gave me replicas of her diamond and emerald ring and earrings as draw prizes. The items raised many hundreds of pounds and the ring, won by the landlady of the local pub, was greatly admired thereafter as it illuminated her hand when she served the customers.

The Molyneux family, of which Lord Sefton was head, acquired Croxteth Hall, one of Lancashire's most historic stately homes a few miles from Aintree, in Henry VI's reign when Sir Richard Molyneux was Steward of the Manor. At the beginning of the 1500s the family lived at Sefton Castle, but that was destroyed during the Civil War by Cromwell's men and they moved to Croxteth.

The Earl (family motto *Vivere sat Vincere* – 'To Conquer is to live enough') had a magnificently illuminated pedigree on vellum seven yards long which traced his descent back 31 generations, to the Norman Conquest. The first portion, which included Crusaders, was the work of Sir William Dethok, Garter King of Arms in the reign of Elizabeth. The Earl also owned the Abbeystead Estate of 18,900 acres near Lancaster.

After his death, his mellow, more democratic, American wife Josephine – they had been close friends of the Windsors, and Josephine's hair, a rich coppery shade, inspired the Duchess of Windsor referring to their friendship in her memoirs, to describe the Countess as 'Foxy Sefton' – looked for an heir to the title, but in spite of extensive research none could be found.

So ended the Molyneux family saga, with Croxteth Hall and the surrounding parkland, woods, and greenery, a ten minute drive from the city centre, being left to the City of Liverpool, for the enjoyment of its residents, and the Abbeystead Estate with one of the finest grouse moors in the country, sold to the Duke of Westminster.

For all his standing, the Earl lost his battle with Mirabél Topham. In 1964 he took legal action against her sale of the Aintree land for residential/commercial purposes on the grounds of a restrictive covenant in the agreement of his sale of the course to the Tophams. The dispute went all the way to the House or Lords and Mirabel finally won the action, after the Lords ruled in her favour. Then the sale fell through.

Mirabel Topham's official reign at Aintree finally ended in 1973, when the course was purchased by Merseyside property developer William Davies for an estimated £3 million. It did not make Mirabel a wealthy woman. Debts had to be settled and shareholders paid their dues. Her wealth at death as reported in her will in *The Times* on December 1st 1980 was £166,602.

Mirabel had always been loyal to her permanent staff and they liked and respected her. Shortly before her 75th birthday, she told them personally why she had decided to retire, quoting the problems of time, energy and money. 'Quite apart from the fact that if I had not been able through their efforts (her niece and nephew) to dispose with a cook and chauffeur, I could not have given all my time, energy and money to the cause of Aintree.

'I am not going to bother you with the numerous tough fights that have had to take place to keep Aintree on the map, but as I have got older and older, things have become harder and heavier until collapse has become obvious. We have not been fortunate in our many efforts to find someone to take my place. To no one but the Tophams will Aintree come as their first interest in life.'

Then came a well-earned thank you for Jim and Pat.

'I certainly could not and would not have tried to carry on if it had not been for my nephew and niece, who have both worked hard and given up so much for the firm. To the permanent staff especially those living on the estate – I should like them to know the reason I came into racing was to help my husband. Those of you who remember Mr Topham will know that he was not a good businessman

– in fact he was a responsibility. The only thing that really interested him was Aintree, but not in a way I had hoped. I tried very hard to change him into someone else which is a habit that some married couples develop!'

She remained at Paddock Lodge until her death. Her niece and nephew Pat and James Bidwell-Topham lived on there until the final Topham link was severed by James' death in 2005 – Pat had died in 1982 – and the Topham connection with Aintree racecourse neared its conclusion.

Prior to his death Ronald had been suffering from diabetes and his weakness for alcohol must have been detrimental to his condition. He was buried at the Franciscan Monastery at Pantasaph, North Wales, where Mirabel would join him 22 years later. His was a private funeral on a cold November day, attended by a small gathering of family and friends. Mirabel, wrapped in furs to keep out the chill, stood with Pat and Jim as the coffin was lowered into the ground to join others of the Topham family. A profusion of flowers topped the coffin with a card reading 'With our love Mirrie, Pat and Jim'.

After a small luncheon party at a hotel, Jim drove his Aunt back to Aintree to continue her reign to which her husband had contributed but a small part.

Ronald had at times sorely strained her patience and although their passage through marriage had not been a love affair without equal, she was loyal and had cared about him. She had a strong dislike for ill-behaved children and those who visited Paddock Lodge, or her Isle of Wight residence had to behave themselves. She could control any misbehaviour with the raising of eyebrows and a steely look from her piercing blue eyes.

With Ronald it required more force, the intelligence to outmanoeuvre him and a sharp tongue from which words would roll to shatter his self-confidence. She was always the brains behind the action and he was the underling. This was shown by the reaction of the Topham family and many people in the racing world, to the news that Ronald had been appointed Aintree chief in succession to EAC Topham.

In her prime Mirabel was a very attractive woman. Ginger McCain, trainer of four Grand National winners – the three-times victor *Red Rum* and *Amberleigh House* – told me that *Red Rum's* owner Noel Le Mare, who had an eye for a fine-looking woman, had commented on this attribute when first they met.

Photographs of her at 30, the age she married Ronald, show her as a woman of great beauty and it was easy to realise how she had caught Ronald's admiring eye.

In his younger days Ronald was very handsome, smooth, debonair and progressed with the demeanour of a man-about-town. He had been spoiled by his mother and it was always difficult to find out the source of his work and income before his marriage and his taking an active role in the racecourse business.

Ronald's mother was disappointed in his refusal to seek promotion above the rank of private in World War I, a stance he maintained although he respected her and was in awe of her authority. He was conscious of her high expectations of the ability of his wife-to-be to fill the role as mistress of his household and told Mirabel to 'look industrious and take your sewing', when visiting his mother.

With her wedding present of a silver ink stand, his mother wrote:

My dearest Ronald – It was a very happy quiet wedding ceremony at the Church and all nicely conducted. The choir was very good and I was agreeably surprised and pleased with both the Church and the Priest. It was much preferable to the Oratory. The Reception was a pleasant homely one and I am sure everybody enjoyed and appreciated Mr and Mrs Hillier's kindness and hospitality. Your bride looked very sweet, her costume was so simple and I hope she got a good lunch on the train to revive her. She must have been very tired with the strain. You did your part bravely and we all thought your speech was quite good.

I wish you both every happiness and joy during all the years to come and may your love and blessings increase more and more. You have had a glorious wedding day to lead the way to future happiness, so farewell with my dearest love, and blessings from the Sacred Heart and Our Lady to you both.

Your loving mother,

D Topham

During their married life Mirabel was often embarrassed by Ronald's troublesome behaviour – as were Pat and Jim. They helped to protect her and they all tried to conceal his hurtful ways behind a façade of his being a 'happy-go-lucky male'. However, his antics were known and talked about behind closed doors. Towards the end of his life Mirabel became his carer and their union was more peaceful and he more appreciative. She remembered him with affection and on the anniversary of his death, the Topham Trio would drive over to Pantasaph to place flowers on the grave of her 'genial Peter Pan'.

CHAPTER THREE

THE TOPHAM TRIO

Mirabel Topham had no children of her own, although her relationship with her niece, Patricia Bidwell-Topham, and her nephew, James (Jim) Bidwell-Topham, clerk of the Aintree course for 17 years, both of whom lived with her, was as close as any mother–child relationship.

Patricia and Jim were the great grandchildren of Edward William Topham, known as 'The Wizard' for his brilliant handicapping skills and ability to make race meetings profitable. He made his mark at Chester before continuing his success at Aintree.

Their mother Gladys Mary Daisy was the only daughter of Edward's son Christopher Reuben Topham, and she held a quarter share of the company's stock. She was a caring person, protecting and acting on behalf of her brother, Percy, who had been confined to a psychiatric hospital since 1922 but who was still nominally a director of Tophams. Daisy – as she was known – married Colonel Edgar Percival Bidwell of the Royal Horse Artillery who died of renal failure in a nursing home when Jim was aged seven, and his sister four.

When Pat was 16 and her brother 19, their mother died unexpectedly. It was an unnecessary loss of life, according to Mirabel, who blamed it on the inadequacies of the local doctor who was treating Mrs Bidwell for blood poisoning. A thread of wire-wool from a ball used in dishwashing had penetrated her finger and she was unable to remove it. Within days the finger became painful, swollen and infected. Her doctor told her to paint it with a substance to remove the infection. But her condition deteriorated, and he sent her to a nursing home near her home in Cheltenham. Had he decided instead that she should go to hospital for emergency treatment it may well have saved her life – in spite of this being before the use of antibiotics.

Jim, who was in the army, received a telegram from the doctor: 'Your mother is seriously ill – come at once.' He was granted compassionate leave and the doctor met him at the local railway station with the words: 'There you are my dear boy, your mother died this morning from blood poisoning.' Jim was just 19 years old.

Having lost their father at such a young age, Pat and Jim were devastated at being deprived of their mother as well.

They idolised both parents but in particular their mother who was always there for them when their father was away on army duties. She radiated a depth of maternal love which embraced them both in security and tenderness. They called her 'darling Mummie', and she had a deep understanding of the emotional needs of childhood. This was evident in a letter she wrote to three-year-old Pat, when she went to London to meet her husband coming home on leave, and leaving Pat and Jim in the care of their nanny at home at Battledown, Cheltenham.

My Sweetest little Pat: Mummie sends you all her love, and big, big, hugs and kisses, and Daddy sends them too! Have you been a good little girl today, and were you good in bed last night. Did you catch some crabbies yesterday afternoon, and are all your dollies and babies very good. Are the Doggies good too. Mummie has sent you a pretty yellow frockie and yellow bathing coat, and a pink coat too.

Did you like the ride in the motorcar yesterday. Mummie
went in the puff-puff to London town and met Daddy. Be
a good little girly, and Mummie and Daddy send you lots
and lots of love, kisses, and big hugs.

This was followed by 24 xxxxx.

In this age of sophistication such a letter would seem
mawkish but the children loved their mother's illustration
of her love for them and when they lost both parents it
made the deprivation that much harder to bear.

Jim wrote to his mother as an early teenager:

My Darling Mummie. I thought I would take this
opportunity of typing to you. How I miss you so. The
place seems funny without you. Do please hurry up and
come home. Have you arrived at Liverpool safely, and are
you alright? Don't forget to ask Auntie Mirrie about the
summer as you said you would. Well I must go now as
my supper is here and I must get on with it. Bye-Bye
Mummie and do come back quickly as I have no one to
talk to as both Pat and Zellie are very busy.
Tons of love and (three lines of xxx) from Jimmie.
P.S. I hope the new gardener will stay with us. No, I don't
think I really want thinner underclothing. I can easily do
without until the summer holidays. I have something nice
to tell you when I see you.

In 1964 Pat adopted her mother's maiden name of
Topham by Deed Poll adding it, after a hyphen, to Bidwell.
Her brother followed the same procedure.

Mirabel was furious when their mother died and when
told that the doctor was 'a good doctor', she retorted: 'What
ever you may think, I know he was wholly responsible for
the death of Mrs Bidwell.'

Ronald – their mother's cousin – was godfather to both Pat and Jim and he and Mirabel collected Pat and took her back to Aintree. Jim followed when Army leave permitted.

After the death of Ronald they cemented their bond as 'The Topham Trio'. Mirabel ruled the 'Trio' with her weight of character and they respected her decisions and authority without question.

She refused to use spectacles, declaring them to be the cause of weakening eyesight and of no benefit whatsoever. Consequently neither Pat nor Jim ever wore spectacles. Latterly, Jim carried with him a large ivory-handled magnifying glass with which to peruse the menu when dining out and at home to read the newspaper. So great was her influence over them that the fact that 'Aunty would not approve' dominated the rest of their lives.

Jim instructed his tailor always to use buttons to fasten the front of his trousers as Aunt had told him that a zip was dangerous and could cause serious injury.

It was only during the Grand National meeting that a coloured television was rented for the benefit of the Tophams' guests. This was returned the day after the meeting, the black and white television remaining at Paddock Lodge thereafter. Mirabel was adamant that a colour set would ruin their eyesight.

They preferred to live, work and relax together with little outside intrusion; Pat and Jim always under the control of their mentor. Only a few close and trusted friends who understood the boundaries of the family relationship were invited to become part of the Tophams united link. One of these was their much-loved Jack Russell, Topper.

He held family status. Mirabel was 'Granny', Pat 'Mum' and Jim 'Dad'. To the cleaning woman at Paddock Lodge, he was 'Little Top', and the other family members: 'Mrs Top, Mr Top, and Miss Top.'

Any friendly overtures from an outside source would be discreetly but thoroughly researched by Mirabel pending her approval. The result was that Jim never had a girlfriend nor his sister a long-term boyfriend. In fact, the one possibility in Pat's life of a romantic liaison, with Cedric a farmer she met during 1957 in London, was brought to an end before fulfilment under Mirabel's manipulative influence.

She loved her nephew and niece dearly and her need to control their lives stemmed from her own insecurity at the thought of being dispossessed of their support and company. They were totally dependable, and provided her with affection, loyalty and constancy, the qualities sadly lacking in her husband. Even when Ronald was alive they were never the 'Topham Foursome'.

Each evening, before retiring for the night, Pat and Jim sat each side of their Aunt's bed, with Topper snuggling on the eiderdown, to gossip about the day's happenings and plan for the morrow. It was a companionship which remained with them all their lives together. Mirabel was happy in the role of surrogate mother but forgot, at times, that Pat and Jim were adults.

Pat and Jim also had their uses within the household. Pat was a brilliant cook and had studied a housewifery course at which she excelled. Each morning she would visit Mirabel's study to receive the menus for that day – whether or not they were entertaining – and to prepare a shopping list. She would then telephone her requirements for Paddock Lodge delivery, to the butcher, fishmonger and greengrocer, or she might walk across the racecourse with Topper at her heels to their farm to collect a couple of chickens which she would pluck and dress for the main meal.

Peter Dimmock once remarked to Mirabel; 'Pat works

very hard. She is always in the kitchen.' Mirabel replied: 'Well she likes it.'

Jim was the chauffeur, wine waiter and 'stoker'. To the Earl and Countess of Sefton, who were occasional guests of honour for lunch at Paddock Lodge, he was 'Mirabel's butler'. Lady Sefton was always amused at how dutifully Jim attended to their every requirement with deference and butler-like perfection, under the watchful eye of his Aunt. She impishly told a friend: 'I would give him a job as a butler at Croxteth Hall any time.'

Jim was responsible for lighting and topping up the log fires that reduced the penetrating chill of Paddock Lodge. There was a primitive central heating system of sorts but the old boiler leaked and kept breaking down and the family greatly relied on the efforts of their 'stoker' to help keep them warm.

When the frost carpeted the racecourse outside, the kindred trio grouped around the fire, at ease in their own company, to enjoy a selection of old musical ballads played on a pianola and dwell on past recollections steeped in nostalgia. Their favourite record, played frequently, was of Jose Carreras singing *O Sole Mio*. It reminded them of when, en route from Doncaster races, they always stopped for dinner at the Palace Hotel, Buxton.

They would be greeted warmly by the manager, Mr Hewitt, who escorted them to the best table in the elegant restaurant. The food was superb, the pink lighting reflected a glow on the faces of the women and an attentive manager invited them to enjoy a glass of fine champagne.

A small orchestra consisting of cellist, violinist and a pianist tinkling the keys of a grand piano entertained the diners. Mr Hewitt would come over, bow to Mirabel and ask if she had a request for a piece of music. She usually chose her favourite.

Mirabel had a great love of musical theatre and never forgot her time as an actress and the magic of performance and the music, which accompanied many of the shows, remained with her all her life.

Jim reserved the most advantageous of seats in the theatres at London and Liverpool for the Topham Trio. In the early days – as was expected of those in the best seats – they dressed the part in immaculate evening wear. Mirabel carried a fan if the evening was warm, and reported on each production with a glowing or critical comment and the expertise of *The Times* theatre critic.

She hummed the tunes as Jim drove them home in their black Rolls Royce. At Paddock Lodge, the pianola was stacked with musical favourites and she was a great admirer of the impresarios who staged the brilliant music, words and scores of that day by such as Jerome Kern, Rodgers & Hart, Cole Porter and Irving Berlin. She included in her Grand National day parties theatre celebrities to enjoy their anecdotes and news.

I told her of my own personal encounter with Irving Berlin – a story she delighted in and passed on with relish.

It happened when I was aged 18 a junior reporter on the *Birkenhead News* serving a four-year indentured apprenticeship, earning five shillings a week in the first year; ten shillings the second year; fifteen shillings the third year, and a pound in the final year, by which time I was doing the work of a senior reporter.

For me, every day of my four years as a junior reporter provided a new adventure and the range of stories I covered gave me the opportunity to explore every aspect of life in the town and beyond – and occasionally to meet a famous celebrity. I accepted each assignment with enthusiasm, even the funerals when I would stand outside the church or cemetery gates to jot down the names of every mourner in attendance recalling my editor Freda Gothard's observation that 'names' sell a paper.

The Birkenhead docks were a source of many a good story. Although I don't like heights I would clamber up rope ladders to board a variety of ships from way beyond. One day it was a whaler and I came home with a good story, stinking of fish and a large bag of whale's teeth.

The Cammell Laird launches were much coveted and only senior reporters managed to wangle coverage of these illustrious occasions. I was at the bottom of the pecking order but my moment of glory was yet to come. There was always a superb lunch and the finest champagne. The ladies who performed the launching ceremony were presented with exquisite pieces of diamond jewellery.

I daily sat on the press bench at the Birkenhead Magistrates' court, and gazed in awe at the magnitude of the hats worn by the lady magistrates.

Below brims loaded with flowers and feathers, the women magistrates viewed the hushed and respectful court scene with eyes reflecting total disenchantment. The reserve of the bench as a whole, chilled all before them into deferential humbleness.

The offences then were trivial compared with today... mostly chimney fires, petty theft, drunk and disorderly, poaching and the aftermath of the occasional romantic liaison between a farm labourer from Shrewsbury and a sheep!

Four letter words to be used in evidence were written down and passed to the bench.

Any hint of indecency on the charge sheet, and I was tapped firmly on the shoulder by Chief Inspector Morris, the police prosecuting officer, and told to 'please leave the court as this matter is not fit for your ears'.

I was 18 at the time and obediently trotted out of court bursting with curiosity. I was naïve to the extreme and it seemed as if everyone was trying to protect me.

Most unusually in those days, we had a woman editor who took me under her wing. She wrote a gossip column and occasionally well-known people with a Birkenhead connection would justify an interview on their visit to Liverpool.

On this particular occasion it was Irving Berlin. I have long forgotten his connection with Birkenhead, but there must have been one for Freda Gothard to tell me to go to the Adelphi Hotel in Liverpool and interview this celebrated man.

As she was working to a deadline I had to telephone the story from the hotel so that she would have the information before the paper went to bed. I knew that Irving Berlin was very famous and I was certainly in awe of him. I was also at that time very shy and blushed at the slightest attention.

Very nervously I took the lift up to his suite. He greeted me warmly, was very kind and courteous and responded to all my questions with interest. I was as nervous as a girl on her first date and when I had finished, I said that I had to telephone my editor with the story.

'Use the telephone in my bedroom,' said Irving Berlin helpfully. I thanked him and picked up his bedside telephone. Freda Gothard was waiting for the call and took down my story in her admirable Pitman's shorthand.

'Where are you Joan?' she asked.

'In Irving Berlin's bedroom,' I replied.

'Christ,' she said 'get out of there quick.'

At that moment Irving Berlin appeared at the door and asked 'Is that your editor?'

I nodded, my heart plummeting, wondering what was

going to happen next. 'Well let me have a word with her,' he said. Nervously I handed over the telephone.

'Ma'am,' said Irving Berlin, 'I have been interviewed many times but this young lady here has done a great job.'

He smiled at me as he replaced the telephone. We had our photograph taken together. I shall never forget his kindness. I liked his music but after that I was always a particular Irving Berlin fan.

Another celebrity I was sent to interview at the Adelphi was the bandleader Ted Heath. He too, must have had a Birkenhead connection sufficiently impressive to attract the attention of Freda Gothard. Accompanying the band as a vocalist was a very handsome Canadian called Paul Carpenter. He had been a former ice hockey player, a film actor and had been a vocalist with the Carroll Gibbons' band.

He was suave, sophisticated and charming. After my interview with Ted Heath, I was sipping a cup of coffee when Paul Carpenter came over to me: 'Hi there honey,' he said his blue eyes giving me the once over. 'Come up to my room 208 in half an hour?'

I looked at him blankly… 'What for?' I asked. A look of disbelief flashed across his handsome features: 'My God woman if you don't know what for don't bother coming.' At this point Ted Heath who had been watching from a distance as Paul Carpenter had moved in on me, took me to one side. 'Young lady please do be careful, Paul has quite a reputation with the ladies,' he said kindly.

It took me months to work out why Paul Carpenter wanted me in room 208. Mirabel roared with laughter!

Jim, an excellent raconteur, had a fascination for ghost stories. At the slightest hint of interest he would dig into his mental storehouse of spooky tales, topping up the fire and dimming the lights for greater effect. He would lead in with: 'Now this will amuse you...' He would watch with interest for signs of expectant alarm on the faces around him, and his belief that the present was haunted by departed spirits gave him an air of credibility.

He'd had his own particular encounter with a ghostly happening during his Army service. Billeted in an old country manor house in Yorkshire, he was returning to base with a colleague after wireless and communication duties.

The clock above the stable block struck midnight as they wearily advanced the last half-mile of the driveway. In the distance from the direction of the stables they heard the pounding of hooves of several horses coming towards them. They paused in bewilderment as the sound drew nearer, accentuated by the swish of carriage wheels and the urgent flick of a whip.

They peered into the darkness but could see nothing. There was a gust of wind and the force of the passing presence sent them flying into the hedgerow. Frozen with fear, they remained there until the sound of the horses and carriage dissolved into the night. Intrigued, Jim did some research and discovered that in days long gone the daughter of the squire and landowner had eloped with the coachman in similar circumstances!

Jim was convinced that Lower Alder Root Farm which my husband Jim and I had bought in 1957 had its own ghost. The farmhouse dated back to 1604 – the days of James I.

It was there in part when the Roundheads fought their battle on our top field. Lower Alder Root was a house of great charm and antiquity but without electricity, and it was not until we sold it 27 years later that we realised that every time we flushed the toilet the effluent disappeared into some distant field and a septic tank was brought into use.

Even living by candlelight for those three months I never experienced even the briefest of encounters with a ghost but Jim Topham told me on a number of occasions he could feel an ethereal presence. I suggested that it might have been the spirit of a Roundhead seeking to renew his romance with a previous farmer's daughter having seduced her in our top field: Jim preferred his own version of a spirit-like figure that simply enjoyed our company.

Jim's main interest in life was his collection of veteran and classic cars. During his lifetime he had owned 12, including a 1927 open Bentley tourer, an impressive collection of Phantom Rolls, a 1939 maroon Bentley, a 1948 sea-green drop-head Bentley, a black Lagonda, a British racing green Alvis and a 1921 Sunbeam once owned by the High Sheriff of Glamorgan and built by the Cunard Carriage Company with a specially high interior to accommodate his tall hat. In 1987, Jim, a member of the Rolls Royce Enthusiasts Club, travelled with Topper, in his post-war sea-green Bentley to the Isle of Man, to take part in the club's rally – at which he won the Concord d'Elegance.

He and Topper had also taken part in the annual London to Brighton Veteran Car Run on a number of occasions. It always proved one of Britain's biggest motoring spectacles with crowds of around one million lining the route from Hyde Park Corner in London to the final destination at Brighton. Only cars built before January 1st 1905 could take part.

Jim's closest friends who shared his interest were Brian and Ruth Moore from Hindlesham, Cambridge, who had their own impressive collection of these special cars. Despite having been clerk of the Aintree course for

17 years, Jim had never been particularly interested in horseracing. His interest and enthusiasm were focused on his cars and the activities involved which he shared with fellow devotees.

Brian is a former president of the Veteran Car Club and once a year he, Ruth and Jim, would set off in their vintage cars to meet at Ashwick and explore Exmoor, Jim driving either his open 1936 Lagonda tourer, or his 1937 four point, 3 litre Alvis tourer, with Topper either on the front seat or tucked under the tonneau; Brian and Ruth in their vintage Rolls or Bentley.

They would wend their way through the narrow roads, by the rivers, up the hills and down the valleys, taking in the incredible views and places to visit. They stayed at the Ashwick House hotel, then sustained by a hearty breakfast and a cereal called 'Sunny Jim' set out on their day of adventure, breaking for lunch at a pub at Porlock Weir. Time disappeared into pleasurable hours of companionship and shared interests. It was Jim's only real holiday of the year, a treat that was to provide him with some of his happiest memories to comfort him in his years of desolation after the deaths of his Aunt and sister.

It is difficult to judge in which direction Pat's and Jim's lives would have moved had Mirabel and Ronald not offered them a home and the opportunity to become an active part of their Aintree racecourse family. Jim and Pat's lineage placed them in direct succession of the Topham family tree, but neither were wealthy. They had inherited their mother's shares in Tophams Ltd but at the time had no experience and little interest in the Grand National scene.

Jim, apart from his army training and ability to tell ghost stories, had no training for a career, in spite of – to quote Mirabel – 'having the best brain of the two'.

Mirabel Topham's birthplace, The Barons Court Hotel.

Mirabel and brother Cedric on the River Avon in 1926.

Ronald Topham's favourite photograph of Mirabel.

The engaged couple with Frisky and Frolic.

The future Mrs Ronald Topham.

Mr and Mrs Topham.

Mirabel Topham, ready for action.

An early photograph of the 'Topham Trio', Pat, Mirabel and Jim with their Scottie Jeanie.

All who came into contact with Mirabel deemed Pat's role within the household to be that of cook and housekeeper. Many of the guests at Mirabel's dinner and luncheon parties felt sorry for her as she worked in the kitchen preparing the next course to perfection, while her Aunt graced the top of the table and Jim poured the wine. She was always at Mirabel's beck and call and in the early days must have missed dreadfully the devoted love and understanding of her caring mother. It was not that her Aunt was deliberately unkind. She was tough on everyone, including herself, and had made a role for Pat to fulfil with her own high expectations.

There was only one time in her life when Pat briefly considered an escape route from her restricted lifestyle and that was when, unbeknown to Mirabel, she prepared an application for a job as companion/housekeeper advertised in the *Lady* magazine. She never posted it.

She told me: 'I was low at the time but I could never have abandoned Aunt. Jim and I really loved her but she could be hard on me at times, but she knew that we would always support and look after her, until the very end.'

Jim's tastes and pleasurable pursuits required high expenditure. Pat never went anywhere unless accompanying her Aunt on social or business occasions or to call at a food shop, so her financial outgoings were minimal. A rare treat was the purchase of a new blouse or suit. She washed her own long auburn hair and brushed it dry until it shone like silk before braiding it into two plaits to be wound around her head in an attractive face-framing circle. She had a beautiful complexion and used no make-up unless she felt that an occasion was worthy of a dab of powder from the compact kept in her handbag.

Dining out was one of her brother's main pleasures and he always managed to enjoy the most expensive items on the menu and to match them with wines of equal merit. I gathered from his remarks that his incoming cash flow was not always satisfactory, and in later years, he admitted to me that he had an overdraft at the bank.

His superb collection of cars were being sold off one by one with the money realised gradually disappearing into the melting pot of high living and the durability of his financial situation. He often sent items of furniture, pictures and china to local salerooms, gradually emptying Paddock Lodge of many of his Aunt's treasures. He did have the good sense to channel her library of historical racing books to a specialist who handled such valuable items.

He asked me: 'What is the point of my keeping anything. I have no one to leave it to. I expect that when I go everything left will be binned and forgotten – like me!'

He sold off his father's collection of guns – including one used for big game hunting. Before the days of stringent security controls on gun ownership, he had kept them close at hand to ward off any intruder. When the day arrived for an official police inspection of his armoury he was told firmly that the extent of his collection could not be justified, in particular the big game hunting gun which would have put the fear of God into any ambitious burglar!

Sadly, one of the pictures sold was the Ben Herring watercolour of a top-hatted starter with a field of jockeys ready for the off which had given Mirabel so much pleasure hanging on the wall of her sitting room.

It would have brought considerably more had it been sold at a London gallery or saleroom specialising in fine art but Jim preferred to filter the items in small anonymous offerings to local salerooms. He was aware that he did not always receive their true value but the continual cash flow proved very welcome.

Knowing of my great interest in cookery, he one day handed me a carrier bag filled with musty old recipe books, and recipes written in his Aunt's hand that she had collected during her time at Aintree. 'You might be interested in these – no one else will.' he told me.

The collection included a booklet *Kitchen goes to War*, in which 150 famous people contributed their recipes for a *Ration-Time Cookery Book*. One was from Prime Minister's wife, Mrs Neville Chamberlain headed: 'Men like this dish as well as women.'

It was fish and leek pudding sufficient for five to six people. Ingredients: three-quarters pound self-raising flour or plain flour and 1 good teaspoonful baking powder, 6oz chopped suet, pinch of salt, 2 thick slices of cod or other white fish, 4 or 5 leeks.

Method: Combine the flour, chopped suet and salt to make a paste to line a 7-inch pudding basin. Wash, trim and cut into cubes the slices of fish. Cut the leeks into 2-inch pieces, placing the fish and vegetables well seasoned with salt and pepper, into the lined basin. Top up with cold water, cover with suet paste. Tie up securely with pudding cloth and steam or boil 2½ to 3 hours.

Lady Milne-Watson told how to double 1lb of butter.

Method: Slightly warm 1lb of butter and beat with a fork to a cream. Boil ½ pint of milk, with a pinch of salt, and allow to cool to blood heat. Stir the milk gradually into the creamed butter. Put in a cool place to set – now you have 2lbs of butter!

I know that Mirabel tried this recipe in the early years of the war as it was jotted down in her own personal recipe book.

Another bright idea was how to make Indian tea taste like Chinese: 'If sugar is scarce put a teaspoon of honey into your tea instead of sugar!'

Jim never objected when other friends and I offered to take turns in paying for lunch or dinner. I had, however, learned my lesson early in this arrangement when I suggested that he select the wine. He did, increasing my bill by £50.

He suggested that I might like to join our friends Brian and Ruth Moore to meet at Ashwick and explore Exmoor in their vintage cars adding 'of course you would have to pay all your own expenses' which I would have had every intention of doing.

Mirabel would loan him money and further treat him by refunding the cost of his dinner out with a friend. She told me that the night he had taken a male friend to dine at the top of a revolving tower restaurant in Liverpool at her expense, 'I was shocked by the amount spent.' She indulged Jim more than she ever did Pat.

At Christmas he sent a side of smoked salmon from his favourite source in the Isle of Wight – from where he bought it for his Grand National parties – to Ruth and Brian and me. He found it much easier to send the smoked salmon rather than go Christmas shopping. I reciprocated with a cardigan – his favourite attire.

After Ashwick, one of his favourite parts of the country was Derbyshire and the Peak District. He knew all the quiet byways through the Peak District National Park on the edge of Macclesfield forest and surrounding reservoirs, with all the breathtaking views of the Goyt Valley.

He was aware that I too had a soft spot for Derbyshire. As children, my sister Patricia and I spent much idyllic time on the dairy farm where my Aunt and Uncle lived in the heart of the Derbyshire Peak District. We brought down the cows for milking, fed the hens and collected the eggs, cared for the calves and watched in amazement as Aunty would gently place a newly born rejected lamb in the side of her oven to keep it warm, for hand rearing.

The kitchen table was always covered with a wonderful array of home-made pies, ginger cake, scones, home-baked bread and farm butter. We were briefly evacuated there at the outbreak of war but returned to Liverpool because we missed our parents so much to spend most nights in the Anderson shelter at the bottom of the garden.

So when Jim fancied a trip in one of his veteran cars to Derbyshire, in search of tranquillity and scenic beauty, he would invite me to go along. The excitable barking of Topper often shattered the peace, the Jack Russell perched on my knee with a fine view from the open-topped car of the sheep he sighted in the nearby fields. The sheep looked up startled, preparing to run, but by this time we were half a mile beyond.

When my niece Belinda and her friend Alexandra came over for a visit from California, Jim suggested a picnic in Derbyshire. I prepared the lunch of smoked salmon, potted shrimps, cold duck and apple sauce and salad with raspberries and cream to finish. Jim brought along two bottles of champagne. The girls had never experienced anything like the ride that day in Jim's stately open-top veteran car. We trailed the traffic through Macclesfield, Jim at the helm in his deerstalker hat me beside him with Topper on my lap and the girls squeezed into the rear.

'Gosh, Aunty I feel like the Queen,' called out Belinda. As we slowed down in the town centre, with beaming smiles, they waved at passers by. The traffic thinned out as we entered the Peak District and Jim followed the by-roads with which he was so familiar. A hang-glider hovered overhead and the girls waved skywards enthusiastically, to be told by Jim: 'If he waves back he will finish up on my bonnet.'

I knew of a delightful place perfect for our picnic. I had discovered it as a child and unless one knew the exact location it would have been impossible to find. It was a grass-lined inlet, surrounded by trees alongside a crystal clear running stream. We all helped bringing a rug from the car and the tablecloth on which we spread the delights of our food, while Jim cooled the bottles of champagne in the stream. The sun filtered through the branches as we toasted each other and ate our picnic with gusto.

The area was only a quarter of a mile from the farmhouse where Albert, the bachelor neighbour of my Aunt and Uncle lived. I told Jim and the girls the story of Albert's proposal of marriage, which amused them greatly.

Albert was in the habit of calling on my Aunt while passing with his Border collie Toss, either to use the telephone or pass the time of day. He was always polite and formal, respectfully raising his cap to wish her a 'good morning'. His eyes would linger on the abundance of home-cooked fare and he was always rewarded with a treat from the table.

He had watched me develop over the years from shy little girl to teenager and had treated me with great respect and kindness. I was invited to his farmhouse where he lived alone, to play with the collie puppies and view his pigs. One was called Arthur and trotted after him like a trained sheepdog. Inside the farmhouse he made me a cup of tea, placing the mugs on the bare wooden table and offered me a biscuit.

He would then crumble a biscuit on to the floor near to the table leg and the mice would appear as if from nowhere to devour the crumbs. We both chuckled with delight. This appeared to be his main source of amusement and he told me the mice were his friends.

Albert was tall, inoffensive, a dedicated Churchgoer and of a sunny disposition. The local scarecrow could have discarded his clothes but somewhat distracting was the fact that his head was completely bald as a result of his catching ringworm from the cattle. On special occasions he wore a little thatched wig.

He never indicated by gesture or words any romantic inclination towards me. One day when I was approaching my twentieth birthday, he wrote to say he would like to come to Liverpool, and visit me and family.

He arrived by taxi with a dozen freshly laid eggs as a gift for my mother and shook us all formally by the hand. He was wearing his best suit and on top of his little thatched wig he had placed a bowler hat he wore for church and funerals. My mother provided lunch, which he ate with relish, and we talked politely about the price of milk, the farm animals and that the collie had tapeworms. All the time the taxi was waiting.

Before he left, we walked in the garden and he asked me to marry him. With no malice whatsoever he added that there was a Church Deaconess who had expressed her interest in him and she was to be his second choice. It was an amazing proposal for he had never once kissed me or ever held my hand.

I thanked him graciously for his proposal and told him I hoped that he and the Deaconess would be very happy. He married her shortly afterwards. They had a son who became a vicar and they all lived happily ever after.

There were hoots of laughter as I finished. They had all given me their full attention. Belinda was intrigued: 'Gosh, Aunty you had a lucky escape. Shall we go and see if he is still there?' Jim smiled and looked at his watch: 'We had better be off if we are going to miss the Macclesfield traffic,' he said – much to my relief.

We all helped to pack everything away for the journey to Knutsford, and Jim's special treat is remembered to this day in California.

Mirabel's brother Cedric died in 1991 at the age of 99. He had served throughout WW1 and in his old age, lived alone a hermit-like existence of his choice in an isolated cottage at Watchet in Somerset. On his trip to Ashwick, Jim always visited Uncle Cedric, taking with him a specially prepared food hamper from the hotel and a bottle of brandy. Mirabel had always been close to her brother and they shared the same sense of humour. They corresponded regularly and on August 4th 1966 he wrote:

Dear Mirrie

Greetings from your brother Ced – Here's wishing you a happy day for 7th August (her Birthday). Three quarters of a century and still going strong – with all your own teeth, own hair and carrying your own top weight, that's good going on any field. I am pleased to read from Trixie that you are in the best of health and very busy at Aintree negotiating and dealing with various people – the outcome of which appears to be that the Grand National will be run next April. It was on the radio. I don't have a daily paper therefore know none of the details but feel sure this must be quite satisfactory to you – if so, allow me to send my hearty congratulations. I expect there is a great deal more to settle and I hope for your sake you can achieve this and then enjoy your fine London house and West Ingle at Seaview where you will be free (almost) of care and have time to stand and stare – enjoy life.

I am still happy here at growing my own produce and living outdoors in all but the very wet days, although I have to admit the stiffness of my years is now a handicap to the full enjoyment of the task.

Wishing you the best of luck and much love, Ced

Trixie, Mirabel's sister died in 1986 at the age of 92.

Jim and Pat were attentive to their Aunt's every need. Jim often acted as her escort when the occasion required. Replying to an invitation to the wedding of Stirling Moss, Mirabel wrote:

Mrs MD Topham thanks Mr and Mrs P Stuart Molson for their kind invitation to the marriage of their daughter Katherine Stuart to Mr Stirling Moss at St Peters Church, Eaton Square, London, on October 7th which she has much pleasure in accepting. Mrs Mirabel D Topham presents her compliments to Mr and Mrs F Stuart Molson and wonders if it would be permissible for her to be escorted by her nephew and co-managing director – Mr J C Bidwell.

Jim was delighted to have the opportunity to chat with so many car enthusiasts!

In the summer of 1962, the Topham Trio received an invitation from the Russian Ambassador to a reception at his residence, 13 Kensington Palace Gardens. It was at the height of the 'Cold War' and Mirabel, although realising it was reciprocal hospitality for entertaining the Russians at the Grand National meeting, was nevertheless a bit hesitant about whether or not they should attend. They decided to go out of courtesy and arrived as requested at 5.30 p.m. Their stay and that of the accompanying guests was timed for one-and-a-half-hours precisely. Their party was to be followed by two others: 7 p.m. to 8.30 p.m. and 8.30 p.m. to 10 p.m.

The ornate reception room was crowded with guests and there appeared to be no space for chairs. By then Mirabel was unable to stand for long and Jim went in search of an attendant who brought in a chair from another room. It was all very noisy and animated with an interesting mixture of guests and their attire. There was a plentiful supply of drinks and canapés on offer before on the dot of 7 p.m. everyone was ushered out as the next line of guests waited to be admitted.

As they left, Mirabel noticed Prime Minister Harold McMillan and Home Secretary Rab Butler queuing on the stairs for their turn to enter. She beamed as she spotted them. In 1960, Butler had visited Aintree on an official visit to inspect the Grand National. He was impressed and had congratulated her on the organisation of such a big event.

They recognised her immediately: 'Good evening Mrs Topham. How nice to see you,' said Butler. They chatted briefly before being ushered on. Mirabel turned to her nephew and remarked: 'There you are Jim, we did the right thing in coming if they are here!'

From when she was a child Mirabel was taught the importance of being healthy and keeping fit. Both her grandparents and father, as licensed victuallers, were well aware of the damage to health of an excessive consumption of alcohol. She was always athletic and had the energy and enthusiasm to enjoy most sporting activities. Although never lacking in femininity her readiness to explore all pursuits of interest to both sexes was admired.

The completion of her car maintenance course meant she knew much if not more about cars than her nephew Jim, although she never revealed this to him – fearing she might dent his self-confidence!

Rowing, tennis, a brisk walk in the fresh air, and exercises to keep her body supple were all part of her routine.

Throughout her life she refused to take prescribed medicines and this was a determination she applied to Pat, Jim and Topper the Jack Russell!

Although nearly a century ago there were few such professional medicinal treatments available, to the end of her days Mirabel resorted in times of need to the liberal use of garlic pills and other herbal remedies. To be ill in those early days was a major happening.

A letter from a friend in 1922 told her:

Desmond has somehow or other got scarlet fever, only a mild attack thank goodness. Nevertheless I have had all the trouble of isolation for six weeks, a trained nurse at 3½ guineas weekly, Sanitary Inspector calling, carpets up etc., Elaine did not get it so she and Ronald have gone to Margate and I am here alone for at least another month. Write all your news when you have time. It's quite safe to come along one evening if you care to, but if nervous don't come. Adults rarely get it but children do.

Another of Mirabel's secrets of wellbeing was to solve a problem, switch off and remain cheerful. Interestingly enough we discovered that we both shared the same philosophy. Remarking on the fact that I always seemed cheerful, she asked me once if I ever felt 'down'. I told her I was born during a snowstorm in the early hours of a December morning and the nurse who handed me to my mother remarked that I had a smile on my face. It had proved a fortunate omen, for good cheer and a resilience to equate all of life's joys and problems had remained with me during my journeying of life.

Like Mirabel, I was a natural optimist, delighted to accept every challenge to come my way, happy to meet everyone who crossed my path and to explore all adventures to the full. Mirabel added, 'and we both have a sense of humour – just like our Jack Russells!'

Although she did eat healthily, Mirabel had an excessive

fondness for good food. Later in life it was a contributory factor to an excessive increase in her weight to 18 stone. She admitted to me that food was her only weakness and seemed unconcerned that she had rapidly become – as she described herself – 'a whopper'. Perhaps it was the perusal of her vast collection of cookery books or the temptation of Pat's culinary delights, which excited her tastebuds – she really didn't mind and was happy at this size, considering eating as one of life's pleasures.

She had the good sense to observe the importance of rest. Even when she was at the helm at Aintree, there were mornings when she would remain in bed until lunchtime working on racecourse business and correspondence with papers strewn all over the coverlet, dictating letters to her secretary seated at the side of her bed, with Pat and Jim hovering nearby ready to take their orders, and Topper snuggled up on the end of her bed. It all seemed to work satisfactorily and she kept her finger on the Aintree pulse in a business-like manner from the relaxing comfort of her bedroom.

Pat's special joy and emotional outlet was in the bond of affection which existed between herself and Topper. Her hobby, collecting recipes and household hints which she wrote into exercise books, was encouraged by her Aunt who had her own imaginative collections of recipes and menus dating back to the turn of the last century, pre-World War II, and from during the war years.

Pat's household hints were a revelation as to what was expected of the housewife in those early days. If she had practised all that was written down she would have made an exemplary wife but with little time for Cedric, the farmer she had met in 1957.

Listed under the heading of:
Qualifications of a good housewife:

(1) Usefulness
(2) Organisation
(3) Humour
(4) Justice
(5) Forethought
(6) Punctuality.
The care of table linen, Tea Pots, Coffee Pots and Condiments. Rules for Sweeping: Close doors and windows; take up mats and clear room; have the right kind of brush and commence at the far corner to sweep towards either the door or fire place, sweeping gently and away from you. Sweep so that the corners are clean, burn the dust and remove fluff from brush and put away head upwards, or hanging up. To prevent dust rising from carpets, sprinkle with well washed tea leaves or shreds of damp paper, working in strips, and always finishing the way of the pile. Daily Cleaning of Bedroom: When cleaning out a room work methodically, and divide into three parts. Open all windows, strip and air beds and attend to washstand. Sweep mats outside.

Spring cleaning must have been a nightmare!

Look through the supply of cleaning materials – dusters, brushes etc. Order all things required before starting this cleaning. Make arrangements with the sweep and window cleaner. Have a special washing for blankets, chair covers, cushion covers, eiderdowns, clean out drawers and cupboards, thrown-away rubbish, clean out the rooms at a time when there will be the least amount of discomfort and inconvenience. Dust and wash ornaments, clean mirrors, and pictures, clean and remove small furniture. Have the carpets beaten out of doors or sent to the cleaners. Clean the walls and wash the paint. Scrub the floor and leave to dry thoroughly before replacing carpets, furniture and ornaments.

To her friends and official guests Mirabel's generous hospitality was immeasurable. Food purchased for these special occasions was of the highest quality with no expense spared and guaranteed to satisfy even the most discerning of guests. When they were dining alone the fare was simple, cost-cutting, relying very much on Pat's ingenuity and her imaginative transformation of leftovers.

She told me that Mirabel had asked her one day as she visited her Aunt's bedroom to receive the desired menu: 'Are there any pigeons, dear?' Pat absent-mindedly glanced out of the window. Mirabel chuckled: 'No silly girl, I mean have any been shot. Do find a couple and make a pigeon pie.'

Chicken from the racecourse farm was curried, boiled, fried and made into pies and soup. Left-over joint was minced for cottage pie. Pat produced toad-in-hole (sausage in mashed potato), mackerel in parsley sauce, fish and chips, fish cakes, brawn, jugged (Aintree racecourse) hare and giblet pie. Health-conscious Mirabel always insisted that even the thriftiest of meals be served with fresh vegetables, cabbage, carrots, swede, onions and a pudding. It might be cornflour mould, milk pudding, cabinet or apple pudding.

Guests who stayed for afternoon tea were treated to a selection of sandwiches, ham, egg, sardines, banana and honey, éclairs, fruit or coffee cake. The menus of the day dictated by Aunt would include one for their Jack Russell terrier. Mirabel's sense of values included household items.

She threw away nothing. Household linen was repaired

and underclothes darned and mended. It was not until the final clearance of Paddock Lodge that it was discovered that she was also a secret hoarder. It was a mystery as to which 'rainy day' she had in mind because much of the stuff dated pre-World War II.

Cupboards throughout the house, including part of her bedroom wardrobe, were filled with cases of tinned fruit, meat, salmon, condensed milk, sacks of flour, sugar, boxes of Indian and China tea, jars of sweets which had congealed into jelly, dried fruit in the last stage of fermentation, and cases of wine 60 years past its sell by date.

Whilst living in Warwickshire, Mirabel had been a member of the Mental Deficiency Committee, and had deep sympathy for people with mental problems. This was evident when the Topham Trio lunched with us at Lower Alder Root Farm, and extended the hand of friendship, with special kindness and understanding, towards Gladys, a dormant schizophrenic and former patient from Winwick Mental Hospital, who lived in as our help. Gladys adored the trio – and their Jack Russell which always came with them.

They always enjoyed the stories of her encounters in the outside world.

I suppose living in such close proximity to the hospital with their patients as our next-door neighbours, our fate was destined to be intertwined.

Winwick's main industry at that time was the County Mental Hospital which had opened in 1902 and provided employment for many of the village residents. The hospital was built on a 206 acre site had accommodation for about 3,000 and had two farms.

One farm was within the walled area of the hospital grounds, and the other, Lower Alder Root was a quarter of a mile away on the other side of the lane. Lower Alder

Root had provided occupational therapy over the years for large numbers of patients – 60 at a time would be seen in one field picking potatoes in the autumn.

At that time Gladys was only one of two patients living outside of the hospital, the other being a housekeeper to a local Catholic Priest.

She was the second patient I had to help in the house. The first, Mary, who came on a daily basis, was truly with the fairies and could be quite scary at times. She lived in a mythical world of her own creation, frequently talked nonsense and had an invisible friend.

I was not too bothered about the invisible friend as long as it remained unseen. I was more concerned about her visible boyfriend, a fellow patient called Stanley, and the several occasions I had caught her trying to smuggle him into the house.

One day she told me that my husband Jim had pinched her bottom. I replied that was ridiculous, I had been waiting all my married life for him to pinch mine and he had neither the energy nor the inclination. Her hallucinations became more alarming and as her invisible friend's antics became more erotic I decided to send her back to the hospital where she remained.

Gladys had heard on the hospital grapevine that Mary had departed and called to suggest that she should take her place. Hesitantly I said I would give her a couple of weeks' trial on a daily basis.

She was a well-built woman in her early fifties with a round, pleasant, face and providing she took her tablets regularly, I was assured that her schizophrenia would remain under control.

She was childlike and uncomplicated. I found out later that she had been born illegitimate, fostered out for a short period of time but had been in Winwick hospital for most of her life. She saw me as a maternal figure and at times called me 'mother'. Mirabel found her story of great interest.

After a couple of months working on a daily basis, she arrived one morning with a suitcase containing all her worldly goods and announced, 'I am so 'appy 'ere I have decided to move in.' Could she have the pink bedroom with the distant view of the fields and Winwick Church. It happened to be the most desirable bedroom in the farmhouse.

I was a bit taken aback by her enterprise. However, it was a large five-bedroomed house and I asked Jim if it would be a good idea for Gladys to move in permanently. He gave his usual reply: 'I will leave it up to you, Joanie.'

I telephoned the hospital to check the situation and the doctor was amazed at her initiative. Gladys would not be allowed to live outside of the hospital until she had been assessed.

Optimistically she left the suitcase in her favourite bedroom and returned to the hospital for an appraisal of her mental state. She was warned that her freedom depended on the regular intake of the pills which controlled her schizophrenia. If she missed just one day her mental state would deteriorate rapidly and she would be readmitted.

She was back at the farmhouse within the hour. Beaming with happiness she unpacked all the bargain clothes she had bought at the local jumble sale and hung them in the mahogany wardrobe.

The longer she was with us the more confident she became. At times she was like a bossy child. She assumed the position of overseer and adopted an air of self-importance. She enjoyed answering the telephone: 'Mrs Rimmer's residence,' she would announce to whoever happened to be on the other end. A flicker of annoyance would be apparent if I reached the telephone ahead of her. She was incredibly naive and innocent, having had little contact with the world outside the hospital.

It seemed to be easy in those days for patients to find their way out of the hospital and explore the outside world. Jim found one woman in her dressing gown asleep between the rows of potato drills in the top field.

On another occasion, Gladys returned home from her Sunday afternoon social visit to the hospital to tell me that en route she met a woman patient in the lane walking away from the hospital. 'She told me her name was Myrtle and that she was going to commit suicide and could I tell her the way to the canal?'

'What did you say to her, Gladys?'

'I told her go straight down the hill and it's first right over the railway bridge.'

We never knew quite what to expect on our return after a few hours away from the farm leaving Gladys in charge. With a childlike innocence she believed every story told to her. We returned one afternoon to find an animated Gladys wearing an outsize man's jumper of rainbow colours similar to one I had seen on sale for a few pounds on a Warrington market stall.

'Do you like it?' she called out before we got out of the car. 'We've had a visit from an Indian Holy man.' Jim groaned. My heart sank.

'He told me my fortune and said I was going to be very lucky. He was very kind and because he liked me let me have this jumper as a real bargain – only fifty pounds.'

Gladys spent very little money and kept a nest egg, which included her pension and the money we gave her weekly, in a tin box in her bedroom.

Still bubbling with excitement she went on: 'He's promised to come and visit me again.'

'If he comes again, Gladys, ask him to tell Mr Rimmer's fortune,' I said.

The highlight of the week for Gladys was our lunch or dinner party. She was sociable to the extreme – all my friends, including the Topham Trio, were her bosom buddies. She threw her arms around the neck of each guest, kissing them with embarrassing enthusiasm. She called them by their first name and held out an eager hand for the gifts of chocolates or talcum powder usually brought with them.

On the day of the party she was out of bed at 6 a.m. and within minutes had put on her best dress, an elaborate array of costume jewellery and was in full make-up. She was always heavily perfumed and when I admired the fragrance she told me cheerfully she had found the bottle on my dressing table! Meanwhile my husband disappeared into his snug to read the Sunday newspapers and watch television – 'Give me a call when they arrive.'

Gladys prepared the vegetables and I did the cooking.

When the guests departed they thanked her for lunch and she beamed with pride, grasping each person in a bear-like hug, kissing them warmly and telling them to come again. To the men she would say: 'If you can't be good be careful.' Heaven only knows where that came from because she hadn't a clue what it meant.

Weekend guests were a particular joy as she was always financially rewarded with a generous note being pressed into the palm of her hand on their departure.

We had one elderly couple, a retired Colonel and his wife, who stayed for weekends during the shooting season.

They were an affable couple but their visits did require a certain observance of the rules of manners. I gave Gladys a pep talk on the importance of respecting one's elders and the need to refer to our guests as Mr and Mrs. She nodded solemnly. When they arrived she called them Mr and Mrs but insisted on giving them a hug, omitting the kiss. Everything seemed to be going well until the next day.

The Colonel had a weak bladder and always requested that a chamber pot be placed in his bedroom. The following morning we were seated at the dining room table enjoying a cooked breakfast when Gladys, ever anxious to please, burst into the room and smiling broadly at the Colonel announced: 'Bertie, I have emptied your chamber pot.' I froze in horror.

'Thank you,' said Bertie. Gladys disappeared on a high, delighted that she had been so efficient. I offered Bertie another pork sausage and humbly apologised, 'I am so sorry. I am afraid that Gladys is very childlike.'

They were decent enough to understand that her mental inadequacies left no margin for diplomacy.

At one time I had been receiving a few indecent phone calls and had tried all my ingenuity to dissuade this man from pestering me but to no avail.

One night Jim and I went out for dinner leaving Gladys in charge. We never left her for long – fearing that she might have sold the farm before our return – so we were back early.

'Any messages?' I asked.

'Oh yes,' she said importantly. 'A man phoned and said, "I've got a big cock here for you luv."'

I studied her face nervously. 'And what did you say, Gladys?'

'Oh, I told him. We don't keep 'ens.'

The man never telephoned again.

This was Mirabel's favourite story and in her thank you letter for our hospitality Mirabel always enclosed a £5 note for Gladys!

CHAPTER FOUR

THE NEIGHBOURS

Aintree racecourse is approximately 15 miles from Haydock Park racecourse. The Topham and Sandon families who exercised their supreme authority over each establishment were friends and colleagues.

They assisted each other with the loan of racecourse equipment – Haydock regularly borrowing the Aintree horse ambulance – and met socially for dinner and luncheon to share the latest racecourse gossip. They enjoyed reciprocal hospitality on important occasions such as the Grand National and special race days at Haydock Park.

They lived like potentates in their own private domains of racecourse acreage, enjoying an important status in the county and must have thought in those early days that their agreeable course of life would last forever.

Each family was an extension of a lineage of clever, ambitious, inventive horse racing enthusiasts who in the past had entered the business by creating their own courses. These ventures over the years had been tremendously successful but as time went by the family businesses at both Aintree and Haydock Park racecourses would no longer be under their control as they fell victims to progress.

Although surrounded by an aura of affluence, which gave the impression of ample means, neither family had the money, vision or expertise to develop the commercial potential of their racecourses with modernisation, enhanced facilities, and increased prize money and it was not a favourable time to explore opportunities beyond the boundaries of racing horses. That line of advancement was in the future when Aintree in 1978 and Haydock in 1982 would be taken over by the Racecourse Holdings Trust now renamed Jockey Club Racecourses. The largest racecourse group in the UK, which in 2007 owned 14 of the 59 racecourses in the UK, they spent £50 million to complete projects and stage racing worth £33 million in prize money.

With this vast input of capital it has changed the racing scene fore ver, despatching the role of many privately family-owned racecourses into the memoirs of turf history. But more of that later.

It would be remiss not to continue the stories of the neighbouring Topham and Sandon families. There is no remaining link to connect either of them with their previous lengthy years of racecourse fame.

The tale of both families runs parallel in drama and pathos. Particularly so with the Sandon family who experienced more than their share of personal sadness, with the Topham Trio giving support and solace when needed.

Many of the courses – such as Haydock Park – were, and some continue to be, run on common land with races staged as part of town fairs and festivals.

Other courses were founded by the nobility for their own private use, Ascot was established by Queen Anne and Goodwood by the local militia on land owned by the Duke of Richmond. It was not until the late nineteenth century that 'park' courses, with patrons having to pay an entrance fee, were established. While the Crown continues to own Ascot and several courses have historically come under the authority of the local council – such as Doncaster

– others in private hands faced the possibility of being sold off – providing the price was right.

Haydock Park racecourse today is a result of 250 years of racing tradition with its origins five miles away at Newton-le-Willows, on an 80 acre stretch of common known as Golborne Heath and the home of the Newton Races which flourished in the 1750s.

Mainly supported by hunting and sporting folk, the racing was free and open to all who cared to come along and enjoy the sport, with a charge for a seat in the grandstand that ran the length of Swan Road bordering the old racecourse. The Royal family visited during the 1700s and early 1800s when Newton racecourse provided some of the country's richest and finest racing of that era. It was known as the Newmarket of the north.

An advertisement for the 1843 meeting announced 'good beds and good stables at all the inns in Newton'.

The main industry in this part of Lancashire in the early days was coal mining, and two mines – Parkside Colliery and Golborne Colliery – were within walking distance of Newton. I was told that in the mid-eighties an area known as Dog Kennel Dam provided a rough circular track near a small lake where miners gathered to see their dogs race.

The Old Newton Cup was introduced into the card in 1807 and is the last tangible surviving link between the original course and Haydock Park. In 1899 the race was run at its new home at a value of £400 and today its value is £60,000, run over a mile and a half course at the annual July meeting.

The history of the Old Newton Cup is almost synonymous with that of flat racing in Lancashire and the names of the various winning jockeys read almost like a recital of the great figures throughout the last 180 years.

Among those who rode in the Newton Cup races on the

old course are Jem Snowden, Tom Challoner and Johnny Osborne. Undoubtedly the greatest of them all was Fred Archer, champion jockey for 13 years in succession, who had a great win at Golborne Heath on a horse named *Anchorite*.

The days of the Newton Cup Races on the original course came to an end in 1898 with the meeting being transferred to Haydock Park on a long-term lease of land from Lord Newton. His ancestors of the Legh family had been connected with the Newton races ever since its inception.

The inaugural Haydock Park meeting was under National Hunt rules and the opening race a modest Maiden Hurdle of £38, over two miles. The most valuable race on the card was the Warrington Handicap Hurdle, worth £136. The 1889 admission into Tattersalls was £1 per day for flat racing and fifteen shillings for National Hunt meetings.

The cheaper rings were four shillings and one shilling, plus one shilling entrance on to the course. Annual membership was five guineas. The one shilling ring was 'The Wide World'. It had no stand, and the catering facilities consisted of one tent housing four barrels of beer. For an extra shilling you could go into the enclosure with its luxury of a covered stand. There was no number frame, just a small board, like a guillotine, on which were hung the numbers of the runners.

Haydock Park is where Lester Piggott rode his first winner on *The Chase* in The Wigan Selling Plate on August 18th 1948 at the age of 12.

The man who created Haydock Park racecourse and founded the Sandon dynasty was John Edward Davies, born about 1836 in Hulme, Manchester, chairman of Manchester racecourse, who on behalf of the newly formed

Haydock Park racecourse Company Ltd leased 127 acres of verdant parkland from Lord Newton in 1898.

He was a man of substance and respectability, chairman of the Sale (Manchester) Council, a Justice of the Peace, secretary of the Salford Liberal Association and, as chairman and pioneer in the development of Manchester racecourse at Castle Irwell, had the necessary expertise to bring success to the Haydock racecourse project.

On December 22nd 1857, John Davies married Ann Phippin in a grand ceremony at Manchester Cathedral, attended by the cream of Manchester society. They lived in Old Hall Road, Sale, where he enjoyed his hobby of orchid growing.

They had three children – two boys and a girl. Their daughter Annis married William Lavender Adshead and it was their daughter Annis Dolly Adshead who in 1918 married Sydney Herbert Sandon who was 11 years her junior and had worked at Haydock racecourse ten years as the course secretary.

He had not been born into racing and spent his first three working years with a firm of brandy shippers, where his duties included trips to the East India Docks for sample bottles for the experts to taste. Part of the job was washing the glasses after they had finished. He told a friend: 'I always seemed to miss the tasting bit in between!'

Later he went into the family building business, acting as clerk of works on the building of the first flats to be built in London's Park Lane. Through his work there he became friendly with the Frail family, who owned the Windsor course, managed Hawthorn Hill and were clerks of the course at Manchester and Haydock Park.

In helping them in an unpaid capacity at Windsor and Hawthorn Hill, he became engrossed in the administrative side of racing, and when the early death of John Davies' son left the Haydock Park secretaryship vacant he was appointed to the post and in due course met Dolly.

The job was not easy in those early days. His stories, recounted to family and friends, revealed an interesting description of horse racing in those years. 'We had neither gas or electricity at the course. There were oil lamps in such places as offices and weighing rooms, and as each horse arrived at the course the lad in charge was handed a hurricane lantern.

'Worse still, we had no telephone. If I wanted to phone the course from Manchester or the course to phone me, the calls had to be made to or from the stationmaster's office at Ashton-in-Makerfield station, half a mile away.

'In those days before World War I, we depended considerably on the railways. Horses and punters alike had to come by rail, and we had as many as 16 race specials from as far afield as Birmingham, Sheffield, Doncaster, Nottingham, Leeds and Bradford, many of them with dining cars, as well as from the neighbouring cities and towns.'

Not the least of transport problems in those days at Haydock Park was to ensure that the horses arrived safely and in good time, and it was a worry for everybody concerned if there was the slightest hitch.

Trainer Charlie Morton, who considered a Haydock race an almost essential part of a classic candidate's preparation, waited with Sydney Sandon on the station at Ashton-in-Makerfield for the arrival of one of his Classic colts. When the train chugged in, the horse box wasn't part of it.

Sydney told Dolly: 'I thought Charlie was going to hit the roof. Although we knew the travelling head lad would take good care of his charge, it isn't funny to have £20,000 worth of well-bred horseflesh, perhaps carrying thousands of pounds of private and public money on his head, to be lost without trace. I got busy on the phone, to discover that they had forgotten to uncouple the box at Lowton St Mary's and the horse was at Wigan!'

With an infrequent service between the local stations, it was more than two hours before colt and trainer were reunited.

Later the building of a train station adjoining the racecourse enabled passengers and horses – with a direct link with Newmarket – to alight there on race days. Large crowds took advantage of the rail link.

Sydney and Dolly lived in a flat above the racecourse offices and entertained friends in the directors' dining room. Mirabel never particularly liked Sydney Sandon. His attitude to women annoyed her and led to many a spirited discussion between the two. He was adamant that a woman's place was in the home because 'females lacked the necessary business acumen to contribute much in the business world'.

Spirited Mirabel told Jim and Pat that considering Sydney had the good fortune to marry Dolly, the granddaughter of the racecourse founder, a union which had not exactly proved unhelpful in his meteoric rise to managing director and chairman of the company, his opinion was 'an absolute cheek'.

He was a large man with an authoritative air and when he and Mirabel went into verbal battle those present sat in frozen silence. Sydney was well aware of Mirabel's disapproval but it made little difference to his attitude, in fact he quite enjoyed his exchange of angry words with his 'Queen Bee' neighbour but confided in Dolly: 'Thank God I am not married to the woman.'

'Dear Dolly', as Mirabel called her, was an exceptional wife, kind, caring and tolerant. She bore her husband no grudge for his disparaging remarks, or the fact that he had never allowed her to become a director of what was after all her family's firm.

When age was taking its toll it seemed advantageous much later on to allow their only daughter Barbara to become a director.

Mirabel considered Dolly a close friend she greatly admired but wished that she would take a stronger line to deflate Sydney's arrogance with the occasional swing at him. The force of Mirabel's tirade would most certainly have reduced her own husband Ronald into cowering submission but to Sydney it was additional stimulation to annoy.

In appearance Sydney was somewhat of a dandy. He was never seen without his favourite accessory – a bow tie varying in colour, brightness and flamboyancy. He rode around the racecourse on *Old Smokey*, his 17½ hands grey Irish bred hunter. The large grey horse, topped by his large master attired in immaculate riding attire, bow tie and flat tweed cap, made an impressive duo commanding the respect of the racecourse workers who would doff their caps in acknowledgement.

He has been described as one of the most interesting personalities at Haydock Park with a course connection for over 50 years as managing director – 46 of those years as secretary.

At times he could be quite amusing and enjoyed taking the focal role as entertainer at dinner parties. He would refer to a small book in which he had jotted down his collection of racecourse stories, which might please his guests. Like Jim Topham he was never short of a tale to tell. Here are two of them.

Haydock Park is famed in racing annals as the scene of the biggest 'odds' ever paid out at the Tote. That was at a November 1929 meeting when a Liverpool woman on looking through the list of 34 runners in one of the races, noticed that a horse named *Coole* had not a single backer. More out of pity than anything else, she decided to be its solitary supporter and placed her bet. The horse won at the amazing odds of 3,410 to 1.

The second story was of a happening in 1947 when on the morning of a meeting an aircraft circled overhead and to Sydney's surprise landed in the centre of the course. Alarmed he hurried to the spot and out of the plane came Steve Donoghue, who had travelled especially from Paris to ride in the first race. He won the event and boarded his plane for the return flight immediately afterwards.

Donoghue's innovation started a new idea and since then there has been a landing strip in the centre of the course at Haydock Park, which is in regular use by both jockeys and visitors alike.

Sydney often recounted his racecourse experiences over the years such as the time when racing was bedevilled by unscrupulous parasites who tried to batten on to the sport. To those in charge they were a cause of great anxiety not only from the point of business, but because they threatened the reputation of a sport, of which they were never a part and were certainly not representative.

'I have heard old-time jockeys tell how at around about the beginning of the century some of the smart boys had so far infiltrated racing that often, when it suited them, they gave certain jockeys riding orders and thus predetermined the placings in a race.

'It was audacious and difficult to detect. But it came to light in one instance when a Liverpool bank clerk was prosecuted for defalcations running into thousands of pounds in one of the accounts he handled. Having "dipped" into the account in a small way, he confided in a sympathetic stranger he met on the train after losing heavily at the races. The stranger, one of the "boys", assured him he could put him in the clear if he would send him money to put on the "information" he received. The clerk foolishly agreed, had one or two winners, and then found the thing snowballing into heavy losses on non-existent "information" he received from time to time. At the trial it was disclosed that there had been a leakage in the gang world about this human gold mine in Liverpool and that he, or more accurately, the account, was being bled by two gangs, not one. The upshot was a spring-clean, a full inquiry and the dreaded "warning off" notices.

'With less finesse, but with far more disturbing effect upon the racing public, the gangs invaded the rings after WW1. Fortunately we escaped their attention at Haydock. Part of the technique was the "protection racket", under which a bookmaker was expected to pay a substantial levy if he wanted to avoid being manhandled or having his day's business ruined by interference by thugs shouldering away clients or upsetting his tackle. Threats of intimidation stifled complaints from the public, but the authorities soon got wise, and steps taken were quick and effective.

'Each course had its own security force, staffed largely by ex-police officers, and, though they did excellent work, it was obvious that they were inadequate to cope with this new menace. So the Jockey Club set up its own personnel department, men with wide experience and knowledge of the criminal types and their methods. With photographic memories, they toured the meetings able to refuse admission to known undesirables and to tip off the local police on racecourse duty to keep an eye on their activities. If any of the "boys" did manage to get into the rings, they were quickly spotted and turfed out.'

Sydney summed up: 'I have seen racing cleared of the

parasitic thugs who jeopardised the comfort of punters so that today a day at the races is often an outing for the family. In fact with respect to the bookmakers and the Totalisator Board, I am happy to hear people say, "I could enjoy a day at Haydock without having a penny on a race."'

An observation which could apply today to Aintree and Haydock racecourses.

Sydney and Dolly were delighted when she became pregnant. In 1919 she gave birth to twins. Sadly one of them was stillborn but a baby girl whom they called Barbara survived. The Tophams sent flowers and their congratulations, and the birth was accompanied by much celebration.

The Sandons were a private family and had little contact with people outside the racecourse fraternity. As a consequence Barbara was a very lonely child. She was not allowed to have friends from beyond the racecourse boundary and it was only on a very rare special occasion that a small chum from school would be allowed to come and play.

She devoted much of her time and energy to *Poppy*, her pony, and rode with her father, astride *Smokey Joe*, around the racecourse every day to ease the boredom. Other times she would ride her bicycle, whizzing around the racecourse roads followed by a flurry of dachshund pets. She helped her mother with small tasks around the flat and when she did mix socially it was usually with her parents' much older friends.

She did enjoy race days with all the excitement, crowds and activities bringing some cheer to her mundane existence. A contributory factor to the fun was when her favourite cousin Bill Hall came over from Cheshire for the racing. They were both teenagers and enjoyed each other's company.

One game they played was to collect abandoned tickets

and check to see if anyone had thrown away a winning number. Occasionally, with shrieks of delight they made a lucky find.

Her parents, busy in their box dispensing hospitality, never knew that Barbara and her cousin were trawling the course looking for abandoned tickets. This was all part of the fun. She was close to her cousin and little knew at the time that in the future he would play an important role within her family.

The Tophams would often be included to enjoy Haydock's hospitality. Mirabel referred to it as a most 'civilised course'. When Bill was not present, Jim would excuse himself after lunch to chat and escort Barbara around the paddock.

Sydney and Dolly had hoped that their attractive daughter would marry Jim Bidwell-Topham, a union that seemed at the time to be of advantage to both racecourse families. Jim and Barbara were always good friends and met quite often socially at family get togethers. He would always be attentive to her needs on Grand National day and when the Topham Trio motored over to Haydock Park to have tea with Dolly, they walked together to discuss the gossip of the day and their mutual interest as car enthusiasts.

His intentions were always honourable, he would present her with the occasional orchid but there was never a spark of romance between the two. Barbara told me: 'Jim was always the epitome of the perfect English gentleman. I think his Aunt has groomed him to perfection but he could only ever have been my friend.' Mirabel was very fond of Barbara but it is doubtful that she would ever have allowed Jim to leave her control, especially as he was such an important part of her Topham Trio.

Barbara had never had a boyfriend before she met and fell in love with Frank Hartley, a cadet in Lancashire

The trio in 1978 with Topper.

Paddock Lodge, the Topham's Aintree home.

The Topham's London home, the Nash house at Hanover Terrace.

Mirabel meets the Russians.

And out they go to inspect the course.

Sydney Sandon (left) of Haydock Park with his successor Thomas 'Tommy' Whittle (photo courtesy Lancashire Life).

Frank Hartley with Frances and Christopher (photo courtesy Lancashire Life).

Barbara and Frank Hartley (photo courtesy Lancashire Life).

*Red Rum comes to visit. The trio and Topper with
the three times Grand National winner.*

Topper sits up for a treat from 'Granny'.

Mirabel Topham's favourite print of the first Grand National.

Topper waits for his chauffeur.

Jim Bidwell-Topham at his 80th birthday party.

Police Constabulary. He had been born in 1928 and was eight years her junior. His father Richard was a detective sergeant in the same force where Barbara was carrying out her wartime service as the personal driver of Superintendent Thwaite.

She was tall, slim, auburn-haired and very attractive in her chauffeuse uniform – a suit of dark green with a peaked hat. Her job behind the wheel was a pleasure and in addition to being her war effort it had been a means to spreading her wings beyond the boundaries of the racecourse.

After the war ended she bought her dream car, a silvery-blue Sunbeam Talbot sports car. She had long since lost interest in *Poppy*. Like *Smokey Joe*, the pony had gone to graze in ethereal pastures.

Frank was exceedingly handsome and there was an instant attraction between the two. They became friends and each day Frank would walk the short distance from his home in Ashton-in-Makerfield to meet her at the racecourse. Their friendship was interrupted by his two years of National Service in Cyprus where he attained the rank of sergeant in the Royal Corps of Signals. They wrote to each other frequently and Frank returned with a proposal of marriage, a sapphire and diamond engagement ring and a pair of made-in-Cyprus leather sandals!

They were married at Holy Trinity Church, Ashton-in-Makerfield, on March 25th 1952. The Tophams sent their best wishes and an expensive present. It was a small family affair. Frank's sister Jean Bridge recalled the ceremony. Barbara was elegant in a two-piece of green and red patterned silk with a pleated skirt. The Sandons had arranged a reception at a hotel at Standish, near Wigan, hosting a superb luncheon and the Hartley family drank champagne for the first time. Jean still remembers how it tickled her nose.

The newlyweds left for a week's honeymoon – destination secret – the bride at the wheel of her Sunbeam Talbot.

When they returned their first home on the racecourse was a caravan. They moved later into White Lodge, an extended gamekeeper's cottage on the fringe of the racecourse.

Frank had left school at 16 to take a two-year course at Wigan Technical College in shorthand, typing and bookkeeping. This proved a great asset for his job at the racecourse as clerk and bookkeeper. He later became clerk of the course and director of the Scottish Bogside racecourse in which Sydney Sandon had shares.

Frank's life as a child and that of his three sisters, Elsie, Mabel and Jean, had been overshadowed by the strict heavy-handed disciplinarian treatment of their father Detective Sergeant Hartley. The children were very close and loved each other dearly.

Jean told me: 'I was always getting whacked for some little thing. One day we were sitting quietly at the dinner table when I must have done something with my food to upset my father. He shouted and lifted his hand to hit me. Frank watched in dismay and said: "Dad please don't hit Jean. Hit me instead." My father hit us both, telling Frank that his punishment was for being too soft. We each had our household jobs and I cleaned all the shoes at the weekends. My father had a shed at the end of the garden with a last for shaping shoes on which he repaired the family shoes and Barbara's.'

Their mother died and their father later remarried. When his father retired from the force, Frank obtained work for him with the Jockey Club, proving there were no hard feelings. However, when he and Barbara had children of their own, Frank, no doubt remembering his own unhappy childhood at the hands of his father, was a loving, caring parent aware of all their childhood needs to play and claim attention.

Their children were, Frances Barbara, born in January 1958, and Christopher, born in February 1960.

Frank doted on them and was over generous with an abundance of treats and presents and they loved him dearly. Barbara was not a hands-on maternal mother but loved them equally.

For the first few years of their life the children were cushioned in the stability of happiness that makes a child emotionally secure. Little did they know that this perfection would have a time limit.

By the time that Frances was aged ten and Christopher eight they had lost both parents.

Their grandmother Dolly Sandon had died of cancer in 1960 the year Christopher was born. Her husband died three years later.

Then Frank, at the age of 37, was taken ill at the office and died of pancreatitis in St Helens Hospital on February 28th 1965. Barbara died on November 30th 1968 aged 49 due to a bubble in her kidney dialysis machine which she had had installed in her home at the 'New House' built on the racecourse at the one-and-a-half mile start.

Barbara had become ill a year after Frank's death. She felt tired and lethargic and found it easier to give in to the whims of the children rather than enforce discipline for bad behaviour. Frank had also been gentle and lenient with the youngsters. He had been their playmate and they greatly missed his company, turning to their mother for amusement and companionship. Barbara found the responsibility of their care and keeping them occupied and happy daunting while trying to cope with a debilitating illness.

She spent time having dialysis treatment at a London

hospital where she was visited by her cousin Bill and the Topham family. It was decided to install a dialysis machine at her home on the racecourse – a procedure rarely heard of at that time – with a nurse in daily attendance.

She tried to compensate Christopher and Frances with masses of toys and gifts which were played with briefly and then discarded on to the ever-increasing heap which had accumulated in the living room.

For a while she continued to bring them over to the farm for lunch. Christopher enjoyed these visits, especially any permitted contact with the farm machinery. He cried and hid under the table when it was time to go home.

They were both very naughty, constantly tugging at their mother demanding to know what would be their present on the way home. I devised a plan to give Barbara a rest. She had a nap after lunch whilst I walked the children down the fields to a copse to look for rabbits and play hide and seek. This helped to reduce some of their childish exuberance but most successful of all in my behaviour control of Christopher was a promise that if he behaved he would be allowed to sit on a tractor at the end of the visit. This always worked and gave his mother some peace.

Christopher was always interested in cars, tractors, balers and combines. Harvest time on the farm was the zenith of his delight. Anything motorised consumed his total interest.

He was a friendly little boy and found solace following the racecourse staff at work. Fred Goode, the then head groundsman, who lived with his wife, Annie, and sons, John and Neville, in the house at the entrance of the racecourse, was his special friend.

Christopher would hang around for a ride in the Land Rover and listen to stories about the countryside. Fred

– with a background of four generations of gamekeepers
– had come from Newmarket and there was not much he
did not know about the delights of the land. Christopher
tagged along at every opportunity and still recalls with
interest inspecting Fred's shed containing an array of
dead rabbits.

Fred's son John told me: 'Christopher was a pleasant
little boy and spent a lot of time looking for company after
the death of his father. He was lonely and it wasn't much
fun having the whole of a racecourse as a playground
but no children to share it with. We were all very fond of
him.'

John was nine and living on the racecourse with his
brother Neville and parents at the start of the Second
World War. The Goode family were witness to all the
activity and extraordinary happenings of a racecourse
in wartime. Racing had been abandoned and the course
taken over for military purposes with troops from all the
Allied Nations being quartered there.

The stables became barracks with two double bunks in
each and hastily erected Nissen huts provided extensive
accommodation. The racecourse roads were lined with
Jeeps, trucks and ambulances and the centre of the
racecourse stacked, three levels in height, with cased
gliders. A few miles away, the Liverpool Ice Skating
Rink complex was made use of as a huge freezer to store
perishable items from America.

John vividly remembers the first troops to arrive. They
were the Seaforth Highlanders accompanied by their own
Piper who awoke them – and the Goode family – at the
crack of dawn with the skirl of his bagpipes.

They were followed by the Poles, Czechs, French and
the Americans.

Fred, with his sound perception and knowledge of the

countryside and its inhabitants, detected that the French had cleared all the ditches of frogs – to supplement their diet with a delicacy much appreciated in their country!

Fred and his two sons had a lucky escape one morning when digging in their garden and narrowly escaped being eliminated by two American Military Policemen looking for a prisoner who had escaped from their detention centre. They had taken aim as the bobbing heads of the Goode family appeared above the hedge. As bits of hedge flew in all directions the three dived earthwards to lay flat on the ground. 'Sorry folks,' said one of the guards, 'we thought you might be our escaped prisoner.'

As the son of a gamekeeper, Fred was a crack shot and thanked the Lord that the two American guards lacked his expertise.

The regime of the Military Police and their prison on the base shocked the Goode family. One prisoner hanged himself and another was shot in the neck as he tried to escape. One punishment administered was to bind tightly with thick heavy bandages the legs of a prisoner and make him run with a wheelbarrow until the point of collapse. Guards were told to shoot to kill and were asked to pay for wasted ammunition. John told me, 'They were a tough brutal lot and showed no mercy to offenders.'

Following his death in 1979 after 50 years service, the Goode family buried Fred's ashes at the starting post where he used to stand at every race meeting.

The staff were particularly kind, the cleaners and stable hands encouraging Christopher to chat and assist them. Barbara had a number of people to help with the children including Tilly, her household help.

The children were experiencing the same degree of loneliness as their mother had before them. 'The family had always kept to themselves and this reflected on the children'. I was told. This was evident one weekend when the local Pony Club held their camp at the racecourse.

A group of children and their ponies, under supervision, enjoyed mounted games, grooming and all the fun associated with children and ponies. Frances, a small Lucy Attwell type figure in jodhpurs and hard hat seated on her pony and accompanied by her grandfather, watched from a distance but was not allowed to socialise or take part, and after a while was led away for tea.

She was an attractive little girl, expensively attired in the pretty dresses that Jaeger made for children in those days. She was always neatly dressed but had no young friends to whom she could show her extensive and expensive little girls wardrobe.

The Tophams, indeed the whole of Haydock racecourse, were in shock at the tragedy which had engulfed the Sandon/Hartley family. Christopher had always admired his 'Uncle' Jim Topham not just because he treated him to the occasional ride at Aintree in one of his super veteran cars and each Easter gave him the largest chocolate egg the boy had ever seen, but also because he enjoyed his wealth of stories and the natural aptitude Jim had to communicate with children.

From the time they were toddlers Christopher and Frances had accompanied their mother to an annual pre-Christmas treat at Paddock Lodge when Mirabel, Pat and Jim made a special effort to provide for them a memorable little party.

There were presents under the tree, fun and games with Uncle Jim and their Jack Russell, and a magical feast provided by 'Aunty' Pat. In his middle forties, Christopher, still remembers the delights of her trifle and the fact that Pat spent most of her time in the kitchen and how Mirabel presided over the proceedings with a beaming smile, radiating her own special brand of affection for the family – her battles with Sydney long gone.

Christopher still recalls at the age of five walking hand in hand with his mother around the paddock and being told that he would have to go away to school because mummy was ill and could not look after him. He promised to be a brave boy but that night sobbed himself to sleep.

Barbara always hoped that Christopher would follow the family tradition and become clerk of the Haydock racecourse. She asked me a few months before she died if I would be Christopher's Godmother and she would ask Jim Topham to be Godfather.

She considered that Jim's experience as clerk of Aintree would be of future help to Christopher. In addition the Tophams had been good family friends and Jim a caring foster 'uncle' to both Hartley children. We both agreed but sadly Barbara died before this could be arranged. However Christoper and I have remained good friends and he still calls me 'Aunt Joan'.

After Barbara's death, Aunt Doris – the mother of Bill, Barbara's favourite cousin and sister of her mother Dolly – came to the racecourse with temporary care for the children while a decision was made about their future. Aunt Doris was a kind, elderly, lady who had helped nurse her sister before Dolly succumbed to cancer. It was not an easy task for Aunt Doris to control the antics of two children who had been given free rein by everyone in an effort to counterbalance their emotional deprivation of a stable family life.

They loved her but took advantage of her sympathetic benevolence whenever possible. Jim Topham visited to help divert their naughty behaviour and restore some kind of control. He felt very sorry for Aunt Doris and always brought her flowers.

He played games and told the children ghost stories. On one occasion he helped Aunt Doris bath them and told me he had never experienced such utter mayhem. He found himself engulfed in a battle of soapsuds, which patterned the walls and ceiling and emerged as soaked as the children. Aunt Doris retired gratefully and left him in charge.

It was decided that Frances and Christopher would live with cousin Bill, Professor of Nuclear Engineering and Pro-Vice-Chancellor at Manchester University, his wife Mary, a teacher, and four daughters – Janet, Clare, Deborah and Alison, at Alderley Edge in Cheshire.

Christopher had been at boarding school in Hoylake and Mary recalls the day she and Bill drove over to collect him. 'We saw this lone, sad little seven-year-old waiting outside the school gates with his suitcase. My heart ached for him.'

He had never been happy at the Hoylake School and they arranged for him to board at a school in Llandudno which he liked very much. An added attraction of living with Uncle Bill and Aunt Mary was that Bill had built his own miniature railway track around the garden, complete with trains, carriages and seats for small children.

Christopher was a kind and affectionate boy and apart from his youthful exuberance was no trouble and slotted in well with the Hall family.

Frances had a number of problems and in the end Christopher emerged the happiest. When he left school, having spent so much time at our farm, he decided to go in for farming.

He went to a dairy farm in Cheshire, living with the family and helping to milk and look after a herd of Friesians.

After a year he left because he had hoped to be driving tractors but there were not many about on a dairy farm.

He was still keen on driving and in the end found a job with this opportunity.

He obtained his Heavy Goods Vehicle licence and applied for a driving job at what was then Smiths Crisps and today is Walkers Snack Foods based at Birchwood, Warrington. For 25 years he has sat behind the wheel of one of their delivery wagons, totally reliable and never late no matter how early the morning start. He frequently passes the boundary of Haydock Park racecourse founded by his great grandfather John Edward Davies in 1898 and where his mother had aspirations for him to be clerk of the course.

He has no regrets. He is happily married to a lovely nurse called Mavis, they have 18-year-old twins Jessica and Thomas, and Christopher truly appreciates the joys of family life after the tragic upheaval of his own childhood.

At the age of 16, Frances married her boyfriend Norman and christened their first child Barbara. They had two more children before the marriage collapsed. She has since remarried and is grandmother twice over to the children of her daughter Barbara. She works in the shoe department of a store in Wilmslow, Cheshire. Neither she nor her brother have any shares in Haydock racecourse.

CHAPTER FIVE

TOPPER THE TOFF

To the outside world Mirabel was a formidable force. Alert, sharp-witted, a keen businesswoman, and the first to admit that she was anything but popular with the ruling racing authorities.

In reality she had a brilliant sense of humour and wit, a warm engaging personality and a marshmallow centre – particularly where animals were concerned.

At Grand National time she received a considerable correspondence from anti-National groups accusing her of cruelty towards the racehorses that jumped the formidable course.

One such letter, in 1959, from a Warrington woman, read:

The Lady in Charge, Aintree racecourse
I listened with interest when you made a television appearance the other day, but regret I cannot remember your name.
After watching the 3.15 race on television and seeing those horses fall, I feel I must write and disagree with you when you said 'the horses like it and the people who say its cruel just dont know what they are talking about.' How can you or anyone else say if a horse likes it? I say it is sheer cruelty. The second fence was the only one jumped over, the rest were jumped through. To me it showed they hadn't the energy to race and jump so many high fences. Please don't think I am one of those fanatics who disagree with horse racing. I am not but would say if there must be fences, two would be sufficient at half the height.

I still maintain that if horses could talk, there would be no fence jumping. I am convinced by your attitude that you have never stopped to think what a fall can mean to a horse. Perhaps you could try and imagine what a fall does to a highly-strung animal. If you can still say its not cruel, all I can say is may God one day make you realise you have been wrong.

Mirabel replied:

Dear Madam: Obviously you are an animal lover or you would not bother to write as you do, and I certainly would not bother to reply. I am sorry my attitude on TV conveyed that of a non-thinking person so far as animals, and especially the horse, is concerned, because it was quite the reverse of the truth.

However, I am rather left wondering if you really understand or fathom what you watch since you say the fences were jumped through. This is not possible at Aintree which makes it so very much harder than the park courses where they have the easy birch fences. I can only surmise you must have seen parts of the dressing come off as some of the horses went over.

It is sad that you know so little about the horse, but I was taught when young not to indulge in criticism until I had taken the trouble to learn about the subject on which I wished to point out errors. I should be happy to discuss the matter further and enlighten you if you would care to telephone, and make an appointment for you to visit the racecourse.

For your information my knowledge that the horses love the jumping is from those who spend their lives handling these animals and from frequently watching them. Yours truly.

There is no record whether or not the irate lady ever visited Aintree for a first-hand inspection.

Mirabel told me she considered the National course tough for horses but not cruel. There was far more cruelty in keeping battery hens and she quoted the example of a 23-year-old horse *MacMoffat* who had faultlessly jumped Bechers Brook ten times. Also, there were the horses who after unseating their riders continued to jump the course!

During my 37 year friendship with the Topham Trio I never divulged to them the reason why, after enjoying their excellent Grand National Meeting hospitality, I did not take advantage of the offer of a privileged seat in the stands with a first-hand view of the racing. I made the excuse that it was cold outside (which it usually was) and I preferred to remain indoors to watch the racing on TV. Like the lady from Warrington, it distressed me to see the horses fall.

Jim, my farmer husband who enjoyed racing and was a keen supporter of both flat and over the jumps, knew the real reason for my preference, and told me: 'What a waste of an admirable seat. Thank God I am an arable farmer with no calves or cattle to send to market. My missus would end up with a bovine zoo!'

He tolerated my efforts on behalf of the local RSPCA with the comment, 'it keeps her out of mischief.' His patience was at times sorely tried and when the telephone rang for the umpteenth time he would remark, 'another mouse with a sprained ankle!'

Mirabel enjoyed the animal anecdotes. One story engulfed her in laughter. Our dutch barn was a magnet for people abandoning animals. Cars would drive up after dark and drop off a frightened dog, cat or litter of kittens. We tried to catch them quickly as they soon became feral. Some dogs would wait faithfully by the roadside, watching very passing car in the hope of the owner's return.

We were situated about two miles from the M62 motorway where there is a large lorry park. For more than a week a German shepherd dog, its forehead plastered with tape from a badly treated injury had zig-zagged across the motorway defying all attempts by the police and RSPCA to capture it. The animal was obviously suffering and I and colleague Joan Abbott decided to try ourselves.

The plan was to discover its route, get ahead with dog food and tranquillisers and hopefully, after it had eaten, stay close until the drug had taken effect. We split up and I set out along the lane which bordered Winwick Hospital, cheerfully swinging a dog lead with a tin of Pedigree Chum in my pocket.

It had come to my notice – via the grapevine – that a woman patient was 'on the game' and in the habit of plying her trade with passing motorists in the country lanes around the hospital.

The sun was shining and I was in an optimistic mood when a car drew alongside and a man, winding down the window, called out, 'How much love?'

He was middle-aged with thinning hair slicked over a bald patch, his open-necked sky blue shirt revealing a gold chain. Spluttering with indignation I retorted, 'Don't be stupid, I am looking for a dog.'

He leered at me. 'Huh, kinky hey?' I swiftly rejoined Joan and we managed to catch the dog but I never did tell Jim that his wife had a market value as a tart in the back lanes of Winwick.

As the date of the National meeting drew nearer, Mirabel had her usual influx of begging letters for free admittance.

These were promptly binned – after all she was a businesswoman making a living. Her favourite recipients for free admittance plus a racecard, were Catholic priests. The Irish trainers and the priests were magnets for each other and would rub shoulders socially. This often proved a winning combination for picking a winner.

Mirabel Topham took a great interest in the welfare of the two shire horses working the racecourse farm and regularly walked across the course to visit them in their stables with sugar lumps and carrots. The mounted police horses on duty over the National meeting were often rewarded with a supply of treats from the depths of her capacious handbag.

Dogs were always her particular favourite. Four Scottie dogs and two Jack Russell terriers (Captain Becher and Topper Topham) are buried under the holly bushes outside Paddock Lodge.

She allowed the British Alsatian Training Club to meet every Sunday afternoon at Aintree's Paddock Field, and the annual Championship Obedience Show was held under her patronage, for this special event she gave a special trophy known as the Topham Challenge Trophy.

All her dogs had impeccable manners and were house-trained to perfection by being put out on grass every hour and not allowed to return until they had performed. Pat or Jim would monitor the procedure, voices raised in hopeful encouragement... 'good boy – good boy.'

They were fed to a high standard on food fit for humans and no tinned food. When a trifle off colour, they were dosed with the sort of good old-fashioned herbal remedies – Shirley's linctus, cod-liver oil, honey and garlic pills – which Mirabel used on herself.

Jeanie was the favourite of all her Scotties. They were devoted to each other. One day when her inebriated husband Ronald raised his voice and hand in anger, threatening Mirabel with violence, Jeanie reacted by grabbing and violently shaking his trouser leg. Ronald became more furious and aimed a kick in Jeanie's direction. Mirabel flew to her defence, whacking him: 'Don't you ever do that again.' He never did. Mirabel usually had the last word or blow as the case might be.

When Jeanie died, her heartbroken mistress was so distressed that she locked herself into her room and sobbed for several hours, refusing all appeals to come out.

She told me: 'We were brought up with animals and I have enjoyed their company all my life. I have always been very fond of them.'

This special affection was shared by Pat and Jim, and all the Topham pets were given family status. Guests who enjoyed Mirabel's hospitality were amused to note the after luncheon treat which always appeared on a Royal Crown Derby plate for the four-legged member of the family. 'Topper's tiffin' she would call it.

There might be chopped-up pieces of sirloin beef, roast lamb or a generous portion of turkey and Aintree ham. Milky coffee was lapped from a Crown Derby saucer and a chocolate mint followed, after which the grateful Jack Russell would sit up quite beautifully to perform his party piece, begging his thanks, much to the delight of everyone present.

The feeding of treats during the meal was forbidden. Mirabel graced the head of the table. Her eyes roved the assembly for any indication of an additional requirement to further satisfy the already satiated tastebuds of her appreciative guests. If she spotted the sleight of a guest's hand indicating that the little chap under the damask tablecloth might be in line for a surreptitious titbit, her eyes would twinkle mischievously and the guest caught in the act of dispensation would hastily swallow the choice morsel, whether or not the dog had tried it first.

A family crisis occurred on July 7th 1977 when Captain Becher, the first Jack Russell to join the Topham Trio, died of old age. Very much loved, he was interred with appropriate ceremony alongside other departed four-legged friends under the holly bushes. Mirabel with her touch of humour had introduced him to visitors:

'This is Becher, Captain of the Sultanas – the Course Inspector's Regiment.' If the guests looked puzzled, which was usual, a smile ignited her blue eyes, a chuckle rocked her impressive figure as she pointed out Becher's black and sultana markings. Captain Becher had been brave, bold and a bit of a devil.

In a letter from Paddock Lodge dated December 13th 1976, Pat wrote, 'It was lovely to see you both for our pre-Christmas lunch here. Becher sends his apologies to Jim for the nip! One gets cantankerous when one's legs are liable to give way any minute. I risk a nip every time I pick him up. He is a moody monkey but we should hate to lose him.'

It was little comfort to my husband with a bruised leg patterned with Becher's teeth-marks. However, Becher had served the family with distinction and they were broken-hearted at his demise. Pat telephoned. They had had a family conference and it was decided that his replacement should be another Jack Russell.

The Topham Trio were already well acquainted with Nippy, our Jack Russell, during their visits to the farm and greatly admired the temperament and appeal of the little bitch.

Pat tearfully asked me: 'Can you please find a replacement for Becher?'

Pat would have been happy to give a home to any little Jack on four legs, but where would I find the perfect pup to meet Mirabel's exacting standards?

I had heard there were Jack Russell puppies for sale at the smallholding of a man who worked as an earther with the local hunt. His cottage and outbuildings were situated at the back of beyond in the heart of the Cheshire countryside.

I had been there a year previously covering a *Sunday Express* story about an orphan fox cub being mothered by a working Jack Russell bitch accustomed to bolting foxes. This particular pair had bonded and were progressing in harmony.

The plan was for the fox, when mature, to be released back into the wild and for the Jack Russell to resume her normal working duties unearthing foxes. The story speculated on the possibility of a future chance encounter in the wilds. Would they face each other as friend or foe?

Having confirmed that somewhere in the barn there was a Jack Russell for sale, Jim, Pat and I drove over and crowded into the tiny living room of the cottage, waiting for the puppy to be brought in for our inspection.

He was white, smooth-coated, with an attractive golden tan circle at the base of his tail, another covering his right ear above his eye and a matching brown mark on the opposite side of his face below one white ear. Never having been out of the barn, or socialised in any way, he was petrified.

He was as fly as the newly-born lambs which frolicked in the outlying fields and equally as appealing. Placed on the floor and squeaking with fright he disappeared under an oak dresser and refused all entreaties to come out and show himself.

Pat and Jim exchanged looks of dismay. Mirabel had requested a gutsy little dog with plenty of spirit like herself and as fearless as the jockeys who tackled Becher's Brook. The quivering little pup looked as if it would bolt at the mere sniff of a mouse and hardly seemed to fit the bill.

We knelt down to peer into the darkness below the dresser cooing and sweet talking the trembling little pup in an effort to persuade him that the grass would certainly be greener on the other side of the fence.

His future home at the present, would in all probability have been a niche under a bale of straw in a barn or loose-box, a sack in a kennel, or sharing a shed, possibly arrayed with hanging rows of dead and dried vermin, furred and feathered, impaled for their misdeeds. Life would be hard but interesting, handling firm and impersonal, with few opportunities to toast frozen pads in front of an open fire.

His insecurity had tremendous appeal, particularly to tender-hearted Pat. Eventually it was her kind words and gentle gestures, which persuaded him to emerge from hiding. She gathered him up gently and he snuggled his nose over her shoulder and into the braids of her auburn hair. The response was magical, the flicker of a tail wag. There were several more cuddles and soothing words before he was carried back to the barn.

Pat thought he was lovely and Jim liked him very much but first they had to report to Aunt to reach a mutual decision although she would – as always – have the last word. On the way back we discussed how they could convince the Queen Bee of Aintree that this panicky little pup was worthy of the Topham name.

Their list of attributes was on the generous side: handsomely marked, a pleasant personality, obviously intelligent (had he not had the good sense to nuzzle up to Pat and win her affections) and the twinkle in his eye could indicate an exuberance of spirit. Pat told her Aunt: 'He is a little nervous but very sweet. I am sure he is very bright and will be easy to train.'

They were all missing Becher, and after several days

of consideration, during which I told Mirabel I thought he looked a promising Jack Russell, she agreed and handed over £20 for him from her old age pension, which was collected on her behalf once a month from the local Post Office.

There after he became the 'pension pup', Pat and Jim became 'Mum and Dad' and Mirabel 'Granny'. He was much loved and destined to serve the family with distinction. His story proves that from time to time even dogs have fairy godmothers who can project the most humbly born puppies into the magical world of adventure, luxury, comfort and the sort of canine Utopia of which doggie dreams are created, and that the formidable Queen Bee of Aintree had indeed a heart of gold.

Once the big decision had been made I decided that Topper should write an introductory letter to his benefactor. It was this epistle that ignited the imagination of them all and led to the hilarious canine correspondence, penned on Topper's behalf by Mirabel and Pat, that followed.

The Barn – July 1977

Dear Granny

I am your little Topper. I measure approximately ten inches in length but expect I shall grow a bit! My markings are white and tan and there are those who regard me as not unattractive. I suppose one could say – with a little imagination- that I am quite well bred, my sire being Mighty Mouser out of Top Hat and my Dam Bright Bee out of Honey Girl.

My dynamo is ticking over promisingly and I could, given the opportunity, prove to be quite a lively little chap. My chums here in the barn do not believe me when I tell them I am headed for the Big Time. Laps around Aintree racecourse before breakfast, romps on the beach with Mum

Pat, Dad Jim and you dear Granny at the Isle of Wight, and when at my London residence, the opportunity to rub tails with all those wealthy little Arab dogs in Regent's Park and perhaps even a glimpse of a Royal Corgi.

Following your instructions I have been inoculated to keep me germ free and the children here have me out each day for a play. I am rapidly reaching the opinion that the company of humans can be very pleasant. Also, I wish to acquire a veneer of sophistication before venturing into the world outside. I am told the London dogs are very worldly indeed and I do not wish to be considered a country bumpkin.

With love and tail-wags

Topper.

It was decided that they would collect him in August en route to West Ingle. A gate from the garden opened onto their private pathway to the beach below. Here the Topham Trio would have more time to devote to Topper's house training.

So it was that on a fine warm day in August 1977, a small Jack Russell left his life in the sticks and headed as Topper Topham for the High Life – with three places of residence: Paddock Lodge and 50 acres of racecourse for walkies, a holiday home on the Isle of Wight and 18 Hanover Terrace.

I first met Mirabel when I was writing a series of articles for *Lancashire Life* magazine on the leading ladies of Lancashire. She was delighted with the story and invited me to lunch at Paddock Lodge. The friendship began from there and the Topham Trio became firm friends of Jim and I. They were regular visitors at our farm and we at Paddock Lodge. I admired her strength of character but most of all her humour. She had a brilliant wit and was really very funny.

For example, to make his Aunt more comfortable on the lengthy journey from Aintree to the Isle of Wight, Jim bought a 1976 Traveller caravanette which he drove while Aunt, Pat and Topper relaxed comfortably in the space behind him. It was custom built and fitted with every possible convenience including a cooker-oven, toilet, fridge and a bed on which Aunt could snooze. The wide windows opened outwardly to allow as much air as possible to circulate throughout the vehicle.

On one occasion, with Mirabel dozing on her bed behind him, Jim stopped at the dock entrance to produce his documentation for the ferry journey. The man on duty peered through the open window and on seeing the reclining figure said sympathetically: 'Has the old lady gone?' 'No she has not. She is still here,' replied Mirabel sharply.

She could also be quite mischievous and whenever the opportunity offered itself her impish humour came to the fore. One particular story had us in fits of laughter. It happened during the planning stage for an extension to her second home at West Ingle. The man from the planning office was particularly officious and had clashed verbally with Mirabel on a number of occasions. Mirabel was a perfectionist and knew exactly what she required to improve the comfort and convenience of her dormer bungalow.

To ease the fallout with officialdom, she decided to try another manoeuvre and invited him for tea. Pat produced one of her exquisitely light sponge cakes sandwiched together with home-made raspberry jam and topped by a generous layer of whipped cream. The cake was placed with the bone china tea service on the trolley in the drawing room.

Shortly before the planning officer arrived, Pat busy –

as usual – in the kitchen glanced down and noticed flecks of cream on Topper's muzzle. She hurried to the drawing room and to her horror found that the Jack Russell had licked away at least a quarter of the cake's cream topping.

Mirabel was delighted. Chuckling with glee she said: 'Pat dear, fill in the missing cream but make sure the planning man has that portion.'

It was a natural progression of that humour which helped to create the imaginary romance between Topper and our Jack Russell bitch Nippy Rimmer. The 'affair' became the source of much amusement and the letters illustrated their lifestyle and in particular, Mirabel's brilliant sense of fun. They reveal a side of her personality far removed from the tough no-nonsense businesswoman who called a spade a shovel and ruled Aintree without fear or favour.

But first I must introduce you to the source of Topper's amour – Nippy, a sturdy white smooth coated bitch with tan markings on each side of her head.

There was nothing salacious about the relationship. Nippy had been spayed at six months and when they did meet a brief sniff by Topper in areas of possible potential was followed by his puzzlement of futility. Their liaison was always purely devotional, a never-to-be-fulfilled romance with nothing more than a flurry of tail-wags and a few frantic licks when the acquaintanceship was renewed after a period of absence.

Nippy, too, had been born in a Cheshire barn. Her mother Mandy had produced five puppies after mating with Aubrey, a Jack Russell rescued by the local blacksmith as a Hunt reject and in danger of being put down as surplus to requirements.

Mandy's reputation as the local champion ratter and mouser guaranteed her offspring a quick sale, and four of them, with attractive tan and black markings patterning their smooth white coats, were sold at eight weeks.

Nippy was plain in comparison and remained the unwanted 'Cinderella' of the litter for nearly five months.

During this time she lived in the barn, hurtling around the farmyard after her mother, dodging in and out of the hooves of the Friesian milking herd, and following the farm tractor on which her mother was perched in a favourite position near the driver's behind.

She became the playmate of Gillian, the farmer's small daughter, and as a result of their mutual trust she was always good with children. Indeed, if she saw a toddler anywhere, she would scamper over, tail-wagging as if jet propelled, to lick the child's hand and roll over on her back for a tickle on the tum. If the child happened to be eating an ice cream or chocolate bar, the treat would disappear in one rapturous canine manoeuvre, which left the child wondering if it had been self-consumed.

On a storm-swept day, my husband Jim and I arrived at the farm to hand over ten pounds and collect our new friend who was soaking wet and liberally splashed with cow muck. The pong was quite dreadful. The farmer apologised, 'I've already hosed her down but she loves to roll in the muck.'

I found an atomiser of perfume in my handbag and sprayed her generously before wrapping her in a towel for the journey home. By the end of the journey we all smelled of a midden, and the stench remained within the vehicle for many weeks to come.

From the moment she arrived at Lower Alder Root Farm, Nippy forgot me and gifted her total devotion to her master. The feeling was mutual. They became inseparable. So much so that I said the next time I returned to earth I would come back as a four-legged bitch and not the two-legged kind!

Nippy was cuddled and stroked, showered with kind words, taken out for special treats, bought doggie chocolates, and treated to something pleasing on her birthday. All I could hope for was an affectionate slap on the rump as I hovered over the Aga – as if I was an Aberdeen Angus!

Nippy had her portrait painted by Royal artist ,the late Terence Cuneo, the legendary 'man of the mouse', who with few exceptions, in all of his paintings surreptitiously placed a tiny mouse. He was amused at Nippy's reputation as a champion mouser, so at the bottom of her painting he placed the mouse holding a white flag! The painting was borrowed for his Eightieth Birthday Exhibition in 1988 at the Mall Galleries, opened by the Duke of Edinburgh and for which the Queen and Queen Mother loaned Cuneo paintings. Nippy like Topper was in illustrious company.

CANINE COMMUNICATIONS
West Ingle, Seaview, IOW
September 1977

Dear Nippy
One minute I am snoozing under a bale of straw in a barn, wondering from where my next bowl of milk is coming, and the next, I am being transported miles and miles away across land and sea to a place called the Isle of Wight.
At first I was besides myself with fright. We have all heard stories about dognapping and the desire by some unscrupulous female terriers to introduce new excitement into their kennels of ill repute! So I sat there quivering in this strange motorised kennel driven by my dad Jim, while my mum Pat whispered in my ear not to be afraid.

The third member of the family is a rather formidable lady who I call 'Granny'. I believe she is the Queen Bee of Aintree some field up North. She is very large, with piercing blue eyes which kept weighing me up from every angle.

'Come here my little man and let me have a look at you?' she commanded, and I was handed over for further inspection. 'My what big ears you have, was your mummy a bunny?'

I thumped my tail in annoyance as I tried to tell her that so far as Jack Russells are concerned bunnies are a pleasantry for pursuit. She must have realised that I was a little offended because she smiled and stroked my head most kindly.

They all seem a bit obsessed with my bladder. We stopped at regular intervals on nice patches of grass so that I could be persuaded to have a tinkle. The old dear told me quite firmly that in future this would be the order of the day and I must not perform this natural function indoors. No one ever bothered in the barn!

I hated the din of the traffic and the vibration, as we were overtaken by other motorised kennels. Then, if you please, we drove into the hold of a ferry to reach the Island. I was petrified and very glad when we finally arrived at what is to be my holiday residence at Seaview. I have two homes here with a view of the English Channel beyond and less than a ball throw away from the sands. It is here Granny relaxes and recharges her batteries before buzzing back to Aintree and all her hard work.

I tried to make friends with some elf-size gnomes on the terrace who seemed to be giving me a come-hither look. I think they are a bit thick because they would not play. They say the air is better by the sea. You should come here sometime and sniff the ozone. It goes right down your throat and preserves the lungs. Mum took me for walkies on shore where I paddled in the gentle lapping of the tiny waves.

They all say I am a good boy and have been perfect at going to bed right from the start. They just say 'Good night darling, sweet dreams, now into bed,' and I snuggle down in my basket under my own initialled fur blanket, near the heating in the bathroom. They never hear another sound or whimper – what have I got to whimper about? – even if they are chatting in Granny's bedroom next door which they like to do to finish the day.

Nippy, this family of mine certainly know how to keep a four-legged friend happy. The grub is superb and well planned to give a little chap like me plenty of bounce.

I enjoy lactol, eggs, milk, fresh meat, fish and puppy-meal. I am never kept waiting for my tiffin – a posh word for 'grub'. Meal times are on the dot.

I adore afternoon tea on the sun deck. Mum is a dab hand at cake making. It is a pleasant social occasion and I listen to the family chat while I consume a cucumber sandwich, nibble a delicious buttered scone and, with a bit of luck, a morsel of raspberry jam and cream sandwich-cake. When I get bored with eating, play and exploration, I like to watch the antics of the mongrels on the beach below. They are quite naughty at times and their behaviour is very suggestive. Mum said I must not enter in their merry-making, not only because I might pick up some infection but their antics could sully my pure little thoughts. So I sit here like a toff in my lovely domain, virtuous, sincere and untainted indulging in dreams of you.

The sunshine weighs down my drowsy eyelids until I find you. We are romping through the woods in the sunshine of Summer, and as the shadows lengthen with the declining sun, we nestle together in the coolness of a nest of fern,

and quite honestly I dont know what happens next but I
awaken with all my toes in a tingle.
Love Topper

Mirabel's certainty that the £20 from her pension for their new four-legged friend had been a wise investment was illustrated in Topper's next letter:

West Ingle, Seaview IOW
September 1977

Dear Aunty Joan
My Granny has been wanting to write to you for some time but she has been worried because I have had a cough and she did not want to concern you. She is a great believer in 'kill or cure' and has been dosing me on her home brews! Shirley's linctus, cod liver oil, honey and garlic pills. My health is improving under her careful administration but my breath stinks.
I have a good appetite and have grown into 'quite a lad'. Beauty is not my strong point, as at first my ears were too big to manage and were mostly inside out or sticking out at the sides, and my nose had pink patches on it.
I was called 'Snoopy' by two wretched little girl visitors. My daddy calls me Tinkler or Sprinkler as I am very nervous and if anyone picks me up or comes near I just cannot help it! I really am very frightened. This seemed to surprise Granny as Becher was quite aggressive and would nip before he said 'hello'.
Granny and I had a heart-to-heart talk and she said that I must not be the first under the bed if a burglar comes. She said my IQ was A1 as I knew my name almost at once and also quickly took control of my basket and collected anything I could carry. I learned the word 'ball' right

away and will go and find it when asked. But my star turn is knowing my daddy's voice on the telephone.

I am now given raw meat and surprised them all the other day by growling and barking at the gardener who said warily, 'he's changing, it wont be long before he starts to chew me up.' Granny looked delighted. I have good news on my nose. The pink has nearly all disappeared with only a bit left. My pet girl is Mum who gets my meals and takes me walkies. We play hide and seek and I squeak with delight when I find her.

I have been a very clean boy from the start except for the weakness of my water-works. I am quick to learn and am happy and playful but Granny and Pat think that I sometimes carry my jokes too far, when I swing on the curtains and furniture. Fairly soon I shall be off to my London residence, a splendid house in Hanover Terrace and more gracious living!

Granny says grateful thanks for bringing us together as a happy family… me too.

With love Topper

Nippy replied:

Lower Alder Root Farm
October 1977

Darling Topper,
So you are off to your London residence, a splendid house in Hanover Terrace and more gracious living!
Do I denote a veneer of sophistication polishing the posture of my little country boy! Will his experiences in the fashionable world of refinement and high society confuse his vision as to the true wholesome quality of an unfallen bitch like me? Will the opportunity to dally in

Regent's Park, with the honourable Sarah Sandringham, a Royal Labrador of quality breeding, lead him to higher pastures of expectation while Nippy Rimmer remains a country bumpkin, a bit of fluff with whom to have the occasional romp when he visits his Aintree residence? All of these quite dreadful thoughts fill me with melancholy. I suppose you realise that you are the pinnacle of my pleasurable reflections and that I am continually building kennels in the air. On a bleak day when the mizzle hangs heavy over God's Little Acre and not a mouse treads the dust in the barn, I rest my head on my marrow bone and dream of you.

Now that you are becoming suave, more handsome – ears under control, pink nose spots in retreat – well informed, a personality taking on the sparkle of champagne bubbles and a connoisseur of the goodies of life, do you still dream of me?

Hopefully
Nippy

18 Hanover Terrace
November 1977

Dear Nippy
Granny says I have grown quite a bit but I am still a baby and full of play. She calls me 'the cuddly boy' with which Mum and Dad wholeheartedly agree. I do get a bit fed up with being told that I am not as good-looking as my predecessor. However, I am one up on Becher as I can stand straight up on my back legs and walk like a human. My Granny, noted for being more candid than tactful, says I am a cross between a greyhound and a pussy-cat, as I run with my back legs well outside my front ones and I can make some amusing 'Meeow' noises if they keep

me waiting, even a second, for 'Toppers Tiffin', which is
not very often. I have a really good appetite and the food
continues to be excellent and of Savoy standard.

Although, I have grown quite a lot and am fairly heavy I
stay on the slim side, which I think makes Granny a bit
jealous, as she is such a whopper!

Glad to say that my cough has gone now so no more of the
old girl's remedies!

I actually caught a rabbit in Regent's Park the other day. I
think it was partly tame as they have them running about
in the American Ambassador's grounds!

Don't worry so much Nippy. You do get yourself
discomposed. Of course, you are my number one girl
friend! Flapping is so unsophisticated. I would not be
honest if I did not admit to a fluttering of a heartbeat as
I survey the quiet confidence of the bitches parading in
Regent's Park, their gem-studded collars glittering in the
sunlight. It is my lucky day if they flicker a flirtatious
eyelash in my direction.

I do sense a North–South divide. All the dogs here
radiate their own particular brand of gentility. There is,
for example, a decided upper-crust inflection in the bark
rather as if they are yapping with a ball in their mouth.
This breeding par excellence can also be observed in
the delicate manner in which the dogs perform certain
duties against a tree. No sniffing around the roots and
an ungainly lifting of the leg for a quick squirt, more a
casual sniff, as if one is appreciating a good scent, before
the gentle easing of a leg in an upwards motion of Royal
Ballet perfection.

The canine fashions here are worthy of a second
glance. I saw an apricot poodle wearing a smart tartan
raincoat, with a matching hood and red Wellington
boots. Then there was this rich American bitch in a

slip-over of pale-blue quilted satin, and I heard that Father Christmas was bringing her a mink jacket! She yelped with a quaint Southern American twang to attract the attention of her mistress who was wearing a ring with a diamond the size of a Good Boy chocolate.

I am hoping for an invitation to one of their parties. A British bulldog who resembles his master, a retired Naval Commander, informed me that there are some first-rate birthday parties to be enjoyed when one has reached the right degree of social acceptance. On one such occasion he had feasted on canapés of rabbit and pheasant, a marrowbone jelly dip and chocolate mice. There was also a chocolate sponge birthday cake decorated with iced sugar lampposts, and afterwards they played find the slipper.

Anxious not to miss out on the fun, I am working hard on my social image. I polish my toe nails each day, stand quietly while mum brushes my white fur coat until it gleams like satin, and I shine my collar by rubbing it along Granny's Chinese silk carpet.

It is so cosmopolitan here and one hears so many foreign barks. I am sorry I am not a linguist, it would be so interesting to be able to converse in their lingo. There is a Chinese restaurateur whose dog only responds to commands in Chinese and a small bitch with an Egyptian mummy. Some of the American owned pets are really pushy, particularly those from Texas. They dine on hamburgers and woof suggestively at every passing blonde on four legs. Try it on a Royal corgi and they could find themselves persona non grata!

I was trailing behind mum in Regent's Park the other day, when I was approached by a large dark four-legged stranger who muttered: 'Dobroe Ootro.' My brow furrowed in puzzlement. 'I beg your pardon,' I replied knowing that Granny would wish me to watch by manners. 'Oh *you do not speak Russian – I was wishing you a good morning in my language,' he replied, looking furtively over his shoulder. 'How very kind,' I said, remembering that Granny had told me that when they had Russian horses running in the Grand National, she had invited their two-legged friends to her box for a slap-up lunch, and they had all been most pleasant.*

'Are you connected with the American Embassy?' he inquired casually. 'No,' I said. 'I am a member of the proletariat but have been elevated into the upper classes.' He looked at me with sad brown eyes and replied: 'Plohoy schastva,' which turned out to be 'hard luck' and trotted away.

Mum took me shopping in that posh store Harrods. The ladies behind the perfume counter looked so pretty and everyone smelt so nice – like Mayflowers in the spring. I snuggled in mum's arms and shared her pride at the comments: 'Oh what a darling little boy.' I came back heavily scented having been caught in the line of fire as the girls demonstrated their selection of perfumes. Granny roared with laughter and said I smelt like a pansy and to wash it off!

I overheard Granny telling mum and dad that I am a dear little chap with a great sense of humour but that I snore quite loudly.

Love Topper

PS I am sending you my photograph.

Lower Alder Root Farm
January 1978

Dear Topper
I hope that your cough is better and that your waterworks are plumbing satisfactorily. No wonder you snore so

loudly after all that medicinal brew. I think I would snuff it!

Your photograph reduced me to a quiver. I can well understand your mum wanting to protect you from the chicanery of the IOW and Regent's Park Lolitas who provocatively lift their tails at anything on four legs.

I too have a slight irrigation problem, although I can assure you that I am superbly house trained. My dribbling is not so much nervousness but a joyful overflowing whenever we are visited by doggie enthusiasts. For example, the dear souls who arrive for an RSPCA fund-raising effort. They float in beaming bonhomie in my direction, all smiles, arms outstretched, hands at the ready for hugs, strokes and pats, lips pursed for the odd kiss. It is hilarious.

The most interesting part for me, apart from the chocolate biscuits and cream cakes popped into my grateful chops, are the stories I decipher from their shoes, tights and skirt hems. They are so funny that my bladder simply cannot take the pressure, as I fall about in glee. Can you really credit that anyone could report a mouse with a sprained ankle? A budgie with a prolapse, and the old lady with a dog she is sure must be homosexual because it keeps doing naughty things with other dogs! My friend, Samantha, the Lancashire heeler who lives with us, and I have a really good laugh.

Master thinks they are all a bit daft, mistress included, and takes to the fields when they come. He also tells mistress not to allow any strange bottoms to sit on his Queen Anne chairs! He offers to take us walkies but quite honestly Topper, this is one occasion that neither Samantha nor myself would want to miss, so we hide under the table until he departs. We reply with our own messages more earthly than ethereal and mistress apologising profusely rushes forth to spray some of the ladies ankles with soda water, which sadly neutralises our communications.

How clever of you to learn so much in so short a time. My master says that Jack Russells are especially smart. I had the most marvellous day recently when I was invited to the pheasant shoot. It was a cold day and the wind penetrated to the very marrow, but my eagerness for the stubble and its joys put a spring into my hop, skip and jump. All the smart-alec Labradors were showing off, sniffing around making a great performance of picking up the birds. I knew they had missed a few but being the soul of tact, I waited obediently with my master, the ace up my paw, for the word go.

They had finished the drive with several of the guns shaking their heads and looking in dismay towards a distant (apparently impenetrable – particularly by Labradors) thicket when master proudly gave me the go-ahead. I moved along, my nose twitching like a water diviner's rod and helped to retrieve all of the birds which they had failed to find.

The Labradors were absolutely furious. One slyly nipped my behind. I didn't care Topper, my ego was flying high, a joy I shared with my master as the rest of the syndicate congratulated him on my aptitude. More glory was to come. I was actually invited to join them for hot-pot in the keepers cottage where I took advantage of the roaring fire to thaw out my pads and enjoyed a drink on the house.

You've got a good dog there, Jim, commented one of them. Master was so puffed up with pride I thought he might pop his jacket buttons. He patted my head and replied: 'Yes, she is a little beauty.'

I suppose you know that I am the champion ratter and mouser in these parts. I do not want to sound boastful but I disposed of thirteen rats, one after the other, when the men were loading bales of straw on to the trailer from the Dutch barn, yesterday. It was so easy. As they popped out from their place of safety I nipped in swift as a swallow, and with a clamp of teeth and a sharp twist of my neck despatched all of them to a celestial sphere. Now mousing is more of an art. A mouse hears instantly, pauses his head elevated and freezes into the still silence of apparent indifference. Anxious not to convey a spirit of enmity I observe him from the corner of my eyeball before moving swiftly into top gear for the kill.

My mousing prowess certainly comes in useful. Mistress has been rearing an owlet which some horrid little lad removed from its nest when it was no more than the size of a ball of cotton-wool. It is a tawny owl and she calls him Henry. At first he was housed in the stick-house next to the kitchen door where there are plenty of vantage points for him to perch. He was a hungry little fellow and mistress had mouse-traps set throughout the farm buildings.

She had to cut up the mice into beak-size pieces and then feed them to him with her eyebrow tweezers. He is a jolly little chap but it gives me the creeps when he reverses his eyeballs to look sideways. It is a full-time job finding him mice and I do the best I can. Visiting friends have been most kind and instead of bringing flower or chocolates for mistress, they bring mice for Henry. Two old dears brought a box of frozen mice they had stored in their deep-freeze!

An owls conversion of food requires an intake of some fur or feathers with the meat, so we augmented his diet with bits of chopped up rabbit or partridge kindly donated by local farmers from wildlife victims of the farm machinery.

One day Henry went missing, we found him perched high on a beam in the loft above the barn some distance from the house. He was delighted to see us and flew down immediately, landing on a lower beam within an arm's length of his provider.

He is now able to take a whole mouse and quickly demolishes all our offerings. The loft door is always open and we hope that he will get used to flying around at night and doing some hunting of his own.

Nevertheless, each morning mistress is up with the lark, and mouse in hand climbs the stone steps up to the loft and calls out: 'Henry darling, breakfast time.'

A few mornings ago she must have awakened an old tramp as his head appeared from a bed of straw in the corner of the loft. He looked scared out of his wits and took off within minutes pausing only to write a chalk message in tramp language on the gatepost. It is not uncommon in these parts for a tramp to indicate the hospitality rating (or in this case the sanity) of the occupier for the information of fellow travellers. I don't know what he wrote but we have not seen another tramp since. Mistress says perhaps his name was Henry!

I made an exciting discovery the other day and my yaps of excitement at the side of one of the trailers, brought out mistress and Gladys, our live in help and doggie Nanny to investigate. Aloft among the wisps of straw nestled a family of twelve newly born rats. Gladys returned to the house to answer the telephone while mistress looked for an empty box and I searched for any vantage point which might be used as a leg-up onto the trailer and a bit of sport.

'Who was that on the phone Gladys?' 'It was nothing much,' she replied cheerfully, 'just the magistrates clerk wanting to know if you would do an extra court. I told them that you were very busy on the farm trailer after baby rats!'

Topper can you imagine this – mistress puts the baby rats

in a straw lined box and drove them into Warrington to be put down humanely by the RSPCA Inspector! Master, Henry and I were very annoyed. I could have saved her a journey; Henry would have enjoyed a cordon bleu meal, and master said not to tell anyone in the farming community because they would think that his farm wife was a bit daft!

With ever so much love, Nippy

Paddock Lodge, Aintree
March 1978

Darling Nippy
Mum took me a walk on the racecourse. She showed me some huge jumps. I stood below looking skywards and muttered you must be joking. I thought for one ghastly moment that I was supposed to jump over them. Perhaps this is where granny exercises. She is still much a live wire, I wouldn't put anything past her! Mum said horses jump these fences and that it was part of the National course. Rather them than me.

We had the most delightful visitor recently, a lovely chap called Red Rum *who is a real high flyer. He has won the Grand National three times and twice came in second. He visited Paddock Lodge at Granny's invitation on a social call with his trainer Mr McCain. I was a bit nervous at first because he was so much bigger than myself – I am barely three hands,* Red Rum *is sixteen hands two inches – but he is very gentle and not a bit snooty in spite of being so famous. When I realised what a friendly pleasant fellow he is, I wished that Granny would invite him in for tea and carrot cake. Mum, Dad, Granny and I had our photograph taken with him.*

Granny gave him an extra special pat and a polo mint.

She told him that he was jolly clever to win the National three times and finish second on two occasions, and that he had made Racing History.

The grown ups were chatting, so I decided that as I was the only other four-legged kind present, that I should make an effort to be sociable. He welcomed my fraternity. 'You are a splendid little fellow, do call me Rummy,' he whinnied in my ear. We had a chat about mundane things such as the increase in the price of oats and marrow bones. He is very well versed on most subjects and particularly keen on music. His taste is wide-ranging but he is not keen on heavy rock or other inharmonious sounds. He plays his radio all the time, particularly when travelling between important engagements. He is so beautiful. I adore the warm chestnut sheen on his coat and wish that my tan splodges were of a similar hue. I offered to show him around but he said that he knew the course like the back of his hoof but thanks anyway!

We had a lovely Christmas. All warm, cosy and chummy. Dad, whom Granny calls the stoker, makes the most wonderful fires which roar up the chimney surrounding us in warmth and a rosy glow. I had turkey and Aintree ham followed by Christmas pudding for dinner, and then we opened our presents under the tree. At first I thought that here was my very own special present – a real tree growing indoors, a convenient port of call for Topper on a freezing night when a visit out of doors to carry out essential duties might end in disaster. I received a super ball and other presents and I insisted that everyone share in my delight with play and romps. Granny is such fun and her witticisms make me want to explode into yelps of appreciation. I try to restrain myself in case she mistakes my verbosity as the start of another cough and I am back on the garlic pills, etc.!

There are lots of things to do here and acres of green paradise in which to romp and explore for rabbits and hares. I saw one the other day. He stopped dead, as if petrified with astonishment, sitting on his haunches. His eyes viewed me with intense curiosity, nostrils and whiskers aquiver and then suddenly he thumped his hind legs upon the earth with a low dull thud alarm signal to warn other such creatures to take cover as there was a clever Cheshire Jack on the prowl. I had tried to keep my eye innocently on a blade of grass just beyond him, hoping he would stay, whilst I planned my next move but sadly the instant our eyes met he scuttled out of sight into one of the jumps.

My folks are all very busy preparing for the National meeting. I am told that there will be lots of four-legged friends around but I shall not be able to go out and play nor invite them in for carrot cake, because they will have a great deal of work to do to earn their oats. However, I shall lie on my tummy and peep under Granny's white tulle curtain in the boardroom, and watch them pass by the window on their way to the Parade Ring. If you were here we could perhaps have a wager with our dog biscuits – you know the sort of thing – winner takes all!

I expect to visit my London residence when the family have finished all their work here. I will write from there and let you know what luck I have in Regent's Park, who knows, I might yet bump into a Royal.

Until then lots of tail-wags and many winks from my naughty eyes which Granny says are sometimes positively wicked, so watch out. I am longing to see you.

Your cheeky cherub
Much Love
Topper

Lower Alder Root Farm
May 1978

Darling Topper
Gladys, our nanny, ate a worm yesterday. It was jolly interesting. Master found it in his cauliflower au gratin. It was about two inches long and had gone a sort of browny colour. Master wasn't very pleased. He fished it out and to teach Gladys a lesson, Mistress put it at the side of Gladys' dinner plate. She ticked her off and said that in future she must wash all the vegetables thoroughly. Gladys was beside herself with laughter. 'Don't be silly, Mrs Rimmer, that is not a worm but a piece of meat,' she said and popped it into her mouth. She has been full of bounce all day so perhaps she needed the extra vitamins! Samantha, my Lancashire heeler companion, gets very jealous if Gladys gives more of her time to me than her. The other day, I sat on her knee as she rocked the chair in the kitchen to and fro singing that Jesus wanted me for a sunbeam. Samantha, who had been shaking Gladys', slipper in an effort to attract attention suddenly looked up and yapped: 'Let Jesus have her.' Topper, I was deeply hurt at such unkindness and shall think twice in future before allowing her even a lick on my marrowbone. Whereas dear Topper, you can have my last good girl chocolate drop – any time.
Samantha enjoys nipping ankles. The breed is called Heeler because they were used as cattle dogs to bring in the cows by nipping their heels! I hate ankles. They are so hard and there is always the danger that one might break one's teeth. My cousin Pepie Rimmer, a Jack Russell who lives at Merryfall Farm, got kicked chasing a horse last week and was carried unconscious from the field. He had to have two teeth removed and was in quite a state. He

also had stitches in his face. He is a very brave little chap and twenty-four hours after returning from the vets, he was chasing the horse again!

Love Nippy

PS It is my birthday on Saturday. I shall be two years old and had been secretly hoping for a party. There are quite a few four-legged friends who would like to come. Samantha and I are very popular, mistress being the RSPCA secretary, and we having our very own lamppost. Samantha wanted to invite her friend, the ginger cat from down the lane. He is alright, I suppose but he is a sissy cat and plays with rubber mice, whereas if he had any initiative, he could catch a few real mice in the barn. I suspect he dyes his hair which is a horrible shade of orange around his ears. Samantha quite fancies him!

I was hoping that you would be the guest of honour but mistress insists we celebrate quietly. I do expect to receive a present and saw her hiding away a box with Boneo wrapping paper. Samantha is giving me a chewy stick. She is a bit mean. For her birthday, I gave her a lovely smelly bone from my treasure trove, under the compost heap. She barely said thank you and it was an antique.

Progress report on Topper from Mirabel:

West Ingle, IOW
August 1978

Dear Joan,
I have been going to write to you a heap of times but somehow seem to be extremely busy – really old and slow. Having three homes is very delightful but three spring cleans have to be seen to! Of course, I am now a real fraud

taking advantage of my old age. I just think of all the jobs that need doing – get them in the order of priority and then sort out who can do them (not me) and see they get done.

Our Topper is a great success with visitors – especially children, whom we seem to collect here – Pat at the moment is quite jealous of her Goddaughter – age eight –, as she and Topper are inseparable. He has some amusing and attractive ways. He sits up (without being asked) by the hour and uses his front feet like a cat. Pat has boxing matches with him. He is a huge success in Regent's Park with his beach ball – gets quite a crowd round.

He can run it with his nose at a terrific rate and when it gets really rapid – he jumps it and puts it in reverse – time and again in every direction. When he gets really tired he will come and nestle with the old girl and he always hangs around at meals and watches to see if I find anything too tough – most obliging. He still adores Pat and goes everywhere with her – except tummy height in the sea – but he screams with delight when she come out.

I fear I have been playing truant from Aintree since early April and am not due to return until mid-October. I leave nearly everything to Jim – who is now quite a shuttlecock – every fortnight he goes up for a week – sometimes by train – other times, by car, I find I tire very quickly these days – however I am lucky to now be in my 88th year.

I do hope you are both well and happy and that we all meet again on my return.

With much love from

The Topham Trio and Topper.

Paddock Lodge, Aintree
December 1979

Dear Nippy,
Thank you for my Christmas presents – lovely chewies and chocolates. I am afraid I shan't get all the good girl chocs 'cos Mum keeps nipping one as they are kept in the kitchen. My Granny says she will grow whiskers if she is not careful.

I think my mum is adorable and I think that yours is very nice too. My Granny is keeping her eye on those raspberries in brandy you gave her… she does not think they are safe with my mum in the kitchen. Not that my Mum has ever got rolling – except of course with me sometimes. But being a young chap I look upon myself as Roddy and Mum as Princess Margaret. We have some fine frolics on the racecourse together but when I go out with Dad I have to behave myself. He is quite a good sport but much more strict than Mum. I know my winning ways. Granny says I am cuddlesome. Well of course she is an antique but quite nice in her way.

What I want is to try my wiles on a girl like you – so let's get together soon – who knows what might happen – here's hoping!

Lots of love and tailwags from Topper.

PS Granny had a burglary at West Ingle, Isle of Wight. The police rang us just before Christmas and said our house had been ransacked! The Chubb alarm had worked but the telephone line to the police was out of order… so the intruder had it all to himself. Aren't we lucky to have more than one home!

Lower Alder Root Farm
October 1978

Dear Topper,
Many tail-wags for the interesting messages you sent from Paddock Lodge on my Masters trousers and Mistresss shoes. The one on the toe of the left shoe was particularly intriguing. Honestly, truly, really, my goodness, well!!! You are a hive of information.
I loved your snippet about that daft little bitch Daphne Peke surreptitiously dropping her hair ribbon in Regent's Park, in an effort to attract the attention of one of the Royal corgis.
The zenith of my pleasurable thoughts, and indeed, pursuits given the opportunity, are always centred on a super little chap, such as yourself. Suave, handsome, well-informed, personality as effervescent as champagne bubbles. A connoisseur of the goodies of life... such as Aunty Pat's grub.
No, Topper, I have not heard the latest record 'Tinkling in the Dark', on 'Dog of the Pops'. Mistress says that the new group the Rolling Bones are far too suggestive for a country girl. I prefer 'How much is that woofer in the window.'
My Master and Mistress greatly enjoyed their visit to you and returned home positively ecstatic at what a topping little Topper you are.
Mistress said you are full of the joys of spring and that you are coming to see me with your Mum and Dad, soon! I had porridge for breakfast this morning. Mistress says it keeps the nip in our Nippy!
Love
Nippy

Lower Alder Root Farm,
April 1979

Dear Topper
Mistress says please do not worry about tinkling on the
corner of her ruby damask-covered antique chair, with the
genuine Queen Anne legs. She quite understands that
you were overcome with excitement and roguish thoughts
regarding myself, being in such close proximity.
A squirt of soda water works wonders, so there will be no
stain or pong left to remind me of you – unfortunately!
I had a pretty rough night myself after you had gone.
It might have been the casserole of pheasant, which you
and I helped to demolish and you so enjoyed. I woke in
the early hours with the most ghastly tummy ache and
dug mistress out from under her eiderdown. It is no
good trying to unearth master he pretends to be asleep!
I shot out of the door and hurried to the orchard where
the grass is more sweet, to eat my fill. An hour later the
medicine worked and I needed to go out again. I nipped
into Gladys' room, but first she had to retrieve her false
teeth from a mug in the bathroom. I was nearly bursting. I
really cannot imagine who she expected to meet at 4 a.m!
I was out a long time and Mistress came along to see what
was happening. She opened the door and nearly collapsed
to see Gladys tinkling in the grid! Mistress said she had
probably been caught short as they say in mum's court
when they are up for indecent exposure! It was a good job
it wasn't a frosty night.
It was wonderful to have you visit me. My heart has been
racing ever since.
Yours ever
Nippy

Paddock Lodge, Aintree
April 1979

Dear Nippy
I had a wonderful time after the Grand National Meeting here. You would not believe all the tasty morsels thrown away by the racegoers. I gave my Mum such a dance as I dived hither and thither wolfing down lots of delicious and questionable bits to eat! In the end she just could not cope with me for speed and strategy and put on my lead which I did not think very sporting of her.
Poor Granny has been suffering from shingles. She looked really bad – and an awful sight with one eye bunged up, lip all swollen one side and spots in her head. I made a fuss of her and kept up her spirits, so she is now on the road to recovery and beginning to look normal again. Pity in a way, because while she was really bad I had most of her meals and now she is beginning to eat better, but I still do well as we are both fond of fruit.
Give my love to my favourite Aunty Joan, and to Uncle Jim, xxx for you
from Topper.

PS From Mirabel:
Dear Joan and Jim
How kind of you to send me those lovely flowers and cheery letters just when I was feeling down and out. I fear I have let the side down and behaved very badly just when I might have been useful at Aintree.
Thank you for your kind thought and asking Pat and Jim to dinner, they would, and I would love them to come.
It would be a welcome change of companionship – shingles makes one anything but cheery!
As soon as I muster up enough ginger I want to get south

*to the Isle of Wight. It would be nice if you could come
down for a few days this year.*

*Topper has been a constant companion and he seems to
know that I am not too fit. He goes under the eiderdown
and gazes up at me – like three black currants, two eyes
and nose – we have grown used to each others' type of
beauty. I am hoping to be normal again before long and
look forward to seeing you.*

With love Mirabel

Sadly the attack of shingles had taken a lot out of the
grand old lady of Aintree, and she never fully recovered.
The months that followed the dawn of 1980 brought a
serious deterioration in her state of health culminating in
her death from cancer.

The best distraction from the dreadful present for the
Topham Trio at that time was provided by Topper, born
under a bale of straw in a Cheshire small-holding and
rising to eminence as their adored four-legged friend.
During the last few months of Mirabel's terrible illness he
repaid their kindness multifold with his antics, tail-wags,
loyalty and affection. He hardly left Mirabel's side and
seemed to know when her joyous spirit was at its lowest
ebb, snuggling under the eiderdown to console her with
his warmth.

Nippy and I both wrote letters of condolence to Pat, Jim
and Topper.

Paddock Lodge
June 10th 1980

Darling Nippy
Thank you for your very kind letter of sympathy.
Yes, I miss Granny very much. It is very quiet without

her, but Mum and Dad say that she will be happy where she has gone so I am content to try and cheer them up. They say I am a great comfort to them.

We all went to Pantasaph on Sunday, to see Granny's grave and say some prayers in the church, after which a nice monk gave us a cup of tea and some biscuits. I look forward to seeing my lovely girl friend soon.

With love Topper

Paddock Lodge
June 10th 1980

Dear Joan and Jim

Thank you both so much for your kind letter of sympathy and for the nice things you said about Auntie which were so true.

Yes, she was a wonderful person, and it was pathetic and distressing to see one who had been such a tower of strength, and who had always given the orders, have to go through what she did. But things could have been a lot worse and she could have been in great pain, which thank goodness she was not, except for her leg early one morning when it went numb from her knee to her foot.

Eighty-nine years is a good age to have lived and Auntie said that she had enjoyed her life especially in her younger days, when things were so different and people too! She certainly would not have wanted to be an invalid for the rest of her life. I suppose all things considered her passing was for the best.

The funeral was on Wednesday last at the Franciscan Friary in Chester, and the interment in the family vault at Pantasaph. I am glad it was such a lovely day like the floral tributes. Jim's and mine were mostly pink carnations with a few red roses in the shape of a horse-shoe.

It is very quiet here now and it will take some time to realise that Auntie has gone and that we shall have to get down to paddling our own canoe.
Love
Pat

The correspondence between Topper and Nippy gradually petered out expect for the occasional amusing thank-you note after they had lunch at the farm.

Topper lived on for another 11 years proving an important source of solace for the remaining twosome of the Topham Trio.

CHAPTER SIX

HOSTESS SUPREME

Until the year before her illness in 1979, when she was not well enough to make the journey from Paddock Lodge to her box in the racecourse stands, Mirabel had never missed hosting any of her Grand National parties.

It was an important day on her calendar – an occasion when she was 'Star of the Show' and when the titled, course officials, celebrities and friends paid her homage. Members of the Jockey Club would visit Paddock Lodge in the morning to pay their respects and share with her a glass of champagne. Mirabel awakened early to put the final touches to her preparation plan for what was always a jolly and enjoyable occasion reflecting the excitement and activity of the important day. She remained propped up in her Queen-sized bed until mid-morning, with Pat sitting alongside with pen and paper at the ready to jot down what culinary items she was expected to contribute to the special luncheon.

Mirabel selected a special outfit to wear for the important occasion. This was usually a calf-length gown fashioned in wool crepe indicating one of her favourite colours – pale dove grey, beige or a delicate shade of lavender – and worn with a matching cape or long jacket. It was topped by an eye-catching hat and when a cold wind brought a chill to Aintree she would be muffled in sable fur. The many press inquiries on the big day were handled by Jim. Her outspokenness and willingness to give a good quote had made her a favourite of journalists. She would laugh at the names she was given during the time she ran Aintree racecourse – The Duchess, The Aintree Iron and the Grand Old Lady of Aintree.

At Paddock Lodge, Pat had nearly finished her kitchen chores and just had time to hurry upstairs and change into her suit and blouse and to pin on her lapel her favourite brooch in gold of two owls sitting on a farm gate. Jim gave the brooch to me after the death of his sister and it is an item I treasure.

Jim would bring around his newly washed Daimler and help his Aunt into the front passenger seat while his sister, loaded with her contributions for the luncheon table, climbed into the rear.

At the grandstands Mirabel used the lift she had installed to take her up to the first floor and her suite of rooms which consisted of dining room, kitchen, cloakroom and the glass-sided seating area overlooking the racecourse with one of the best vantage position for viewing.

She always arrived early to check that everything was in order and to give the staff their instructions. She studied the place settings, noted the cleanliness of the china and cutlery and that the attractive arrangement of spring flowers centrepiece was to her liking. She made sure that all the large buckets filled with ice and bottles of vintage champagne were of perfect temperature. In the hearth a coal-fire burned brightly with a welcoming warmth. She greeted each guest with a friendly smile and kiss and made sure that they were handed a flute of champagne from the bottles in the ice buckets where, as if by magic, there was always an ample supply available no matter how much the guests imbibed.

As a wine connoisseur, Jim had, with Mirabel's help, already selected the most appropriate wine to accompany each course. Racecards were handed out and everyone exchanged views on the chances of their own selection winning the big race.

Mirabel was not a gambler and only occasionally would she ask Jim to place a bet on her behalf – usually for a horse with a name associated with the theatre.

Mirabel's hospitality was equal in quality and choice to that enjoyed in the private rooms of the Earls of Derby and Sefton. She planned meticulously to make sure that everything was perfect but occasionally something happened beyond her control to upset her. Such an incident took place when a sneak thief entered the cloakroom and stole the sheepskin jacket of a male guest. She was mortified and replaced it soon afterwards with a new one.

It was in Mirabel's box on two separate occasions that Russian leader Georgy Malenkov, his wife Elena, a former actress, and their entourage sampled the Topham hospitality. The first time was in 1956 when, inspired by Mirabel, the Russians were exploring the possibility of sending three of their horses to take part in a future Grand National.

Mirabel entertained the advance party of investigative Russians and with the help of an interpreter found them to be courteous, pleasant, and most appreciative of the champagne and highly pleasing cuisine proffered on that day.

On the previous day, at the age of 65, resplendent in an ankle-length purple gown and cape topped with a matching hat trimmed with mink, she had walked the course on the arm of a Russian official, and escorted by the Russian trainer.

The second occasion on which the Russians had the pleasurable experience of being entertained in Mirabel's box, was in 1961, when they were running three horses in the Grand

National: *Relief, Grifel* and *Epigraff.* None had raced before, had top weight and were handicapped accordingly. Ten visas had been issued to the accompanying Russians' party, and Lord Leverhulme, by then a steward at Aintree, entertained them on a separate occasion saying: 'I hope it will lead to goodwill between our countries.'

Mirabel felt sorry for the horses. They had travelled for many days by train overland from Russia and this combined with the Channel crossing had stressed them considerably. Their early arrival, and Mirabel's concern for their welfare, provided the opportunity for them to be stabled at Haydock Park racecourse, to recover their equilibrium and have a practice run jumping the Haydock fences.

The horses, jockeys and their entourage were welcomed to the Haydock racecourse but there was dismay among the observers at the appearance and condition of the Russian mounts. They were not well groomed and to the experienced eye 'looked as if they had come out of a field'. Indeed on their first practice around the Haydock jumping course two of the horses fell.

The horses were bedded down in the stable block, enjoying all the comforts accorded to other racecourse equine visitors. Their handlers stayed in the course jockeys' hostel situated nearby. The hostel had been built for, and used as, an American hospital, during the war years.

Radiating bonhomie and anxious to please, the Russians handed around gifts of Russian cigarettes called 'Sputniks'. They consisted of a cardboard tube containing an inch of tobacco at the base. The Haydock staff who accepted the gift were soon spluttering and coughing! A swig of vodka from the ample supply the Russians had brought with them helped to restore their equilibrium.

A senior official of the group, who had been driven

from London in a black Jaguar, insisted on making the return journey by train – because 'the English go too fast'. It was more than he could say for his horses.

On Grand National day, the Malenkovs were accompanied by the Soviet Foreign Minister Andrei Gromyko and his wife Lidiya. The lunch provided was of the highest excellence: smoked salmon, Morecambe Bay shrimps, fillet of beef, raspberry meringues, Stilton, port, plus a large Havana cigar for the gentlemen. A cigar of such excellence must have been greatly appreciated after the 'Sputnik' cigarettes which even the local tramp refused! Mrs Gromyko spoke a little English and was able to make polite conversation with their hostess but the other Anglo–Russian guests communicated through an interpreter.

Champagne glasses were frequently topped up and there were numerous reciprocal toasts 'Nazdrovyeh – Your good health', between guests and their hostess. Mirabel was amused when one of the Russians interpreted a toast used in his country: 'May you have as many tears in your life as there are drops left in your glass.' She observed pertly, 'I suppose that is how you get young ladies drunk!'

The Russians ate appreciatively of all on offer and during the meal Mirabel observed Gromyko studying her with a probing eye. Jim, her nephew, told me: 'He gave no clue as to what he might be thinking. He never smiled and had this look of profound disenchantment. Somewhat alarmingly he carried a revolver which he moved occasionally from his left-hand pocket to the right-hand pocket of his smart grey suit and back again.'

His wife was more relaxed and pleasant. Mirabel liked her very much and enjoyed her company.

Mrs Malenkov entered into the spirit of the day's racing and backed a horse called *Pippikin*, because she liked the name but lost her wager. Mirabel was impressed with the manners of the Russians, one of whom offered his arm to help her negotiate the bank on the way back to her box.

Before they departed they demolished with relish a sumptuous tea of delicious sandwiches, scones, and a variety of cakes. It topped a day of superb Aintree hospitality for which Mirabel was thanked warmly with even Gromyko managing a bleak smile.

After such a surfeit of high living and generous hospitality it was usual for the over-indulged guests to express their thanks to Mirabel before departing. However, there was one guest who 'blotted his copybook', leaving out of favour, never to be invited again.

He was Colonel Harry Llewellyn who, riding his famous horse *Foxhunter* in the final round of the Olympic Games at Helsinki in 1952, was responsible for the British team winning the gold medal. He was the father of then man-about-town Dai, and Roddy, the boyfriend of Princess Margaret.

Having enjoyed his fill of lunch and afternoon tea, he asked the waitress, within Mirabel's hearing, 'Could you pop some of the left-overs in a bag and I will take them home for supper.'

The hostess was not amused. She might have been more agreeable had he said it was for his horse.

For her Grand National parties, Mirabel stage-managed the guest list and place settings to include a blend of celebrities, close friends, and extrovert characters with a sense of fun who would contribute to the conversation and liven things up.

Mavis Pilkington, wife of Lord Pilkington whose family started the mighty glass firm in St Helens in 1826, certainly fitted this category. A RADA graduate and actress before her marriage, she was intelligent, personable, outrageous, warm and vital, and as Mirabel said 'The men like her because she is one hundred per cent feminine.'

She entertained Mirabel with her sense of fun and was a regular guest with Sir Harry, on Grand National day. Her attire was usually eye-catching, short tight skirts, totteringly high-heeled shoes, amazing hats perched on top of her blonde bouffant hair. Although she admitted to middle age, the aura of youth remained with her and she enjoyed a toboggan ride down the snow-carpeted slopes behind Windle Hall, their home near St Helens.

No matter what time of day she always dressed as if going to a party. I had coffee with her at 10 a.m. in their 18th-century house, a lofty 12-bedroomed, pale-blue, stone building, standing amidst eight acres of garden and woodland. She sat behind a mountain of invitations dressed as if for the party, in a black gown, triple link of pearls, pearl brooch, black patent shoes and on her hand a shilling-size diamond cluster which flashed with every movement.

Topping her pale blonde excessively bouffant hair style was an exquisite tiara, made in 1750, of rose-cut diamonds arranged in two side sprays of flowers with a centre rose of diamond and rubies. It was a special gift from her husband on his elevation to the peerage in the 1968 New Year Honours. She did not usually wear it for coffee but had wanted to show me the present from 'my darling Harry'.

She had a well-earned reputation as a party hostess. In the summer they had weekend tennis parties, and with a wide circle of friends, evening buffet parties, guests frequently overflowed into a large marquee in the garden. Her parties were one of the few acceptable to the Topham Trio. On National day Mirabel always knew that friend Mavis would 'sing for her lunch', and entertain the guests with her stories and humour.

There were not many women who had lit a fibreglass furnace – which to Pilkington's was rather like launching a ship. Lord Pilkington, a reserved and charming man, would quietly look on as his wife held centre stage.

'You must be very rich,' gushed one of the guests, who had read a recent report that the then total assets of the world's biggest glass manufacturers had recently topped £100m. With a wave of her diamond stacked fingers she replied: 'Oh I do wish people would not call little me a millionairess. The money is involved with various members of the family – it's not all ours you know.'

Millionairess she might have been but she was always desperate for a win on the big race and, sipping champagne, would avidly study her race card and a page from *Sporting Life*.

On one National occasion, even Mirabel was delighted by the magnificence of Lady Pilkington's hat. It resembled a coffee-brown, smooth-coated, flat-chested guinea fowl (headless of course) nestling in a cartwheel of coffee-brown feathers tipped with cream – as if it had had a brief encounter with a moulting duck. It really was the most exotic hat at the course that day, and the whole creation could have flown in and made a perfect three-point landing on her Ladyship's bouffant hair. Sparking blue eyes peeped from under the enormous brim and lit up like stars when *Lucius* romped home. She squealed with delight turning to Lord Pilkington: 'Darling, silly little me. I only put pennies on *Lucius*, and backed him because I thought he was trained by that famous Sir Gordon Richards.'

With the air of an over indulgent parent her husband smiled benignly: 'Oh darling how clever you are – but then you always did land on your feet.'

Blowing him a kiss, she trotted off into the Aintree

mizzle, short skirt straining at the knees, high heels tottering, plumage protected and head buried in a canary yellow frill-edged umbrella, unable to see where she was going but guided, as if by radar, to the Tote to collect her winnings.

Back in the Queen Bee's box everyone was grateful for the warmth and shelter. It was a particularly cold and rainy day and the crowd in the County Stand were packed like sardines in an effort to avoid the elements.

Mirabel had her own stock of stories she would recount to entertain guests. Here are a few of them:

The National was won in 1908 at odds of 66 to 1 by *Rubio* an American-bred horse who had worked for some months in Towcester pulling a hotel bus.

After winning his second Grand National in 1870, *The Colonel*, a fine-looking horse, was bought by Baron Oppenheim and sent abroad, eventually to become the charger of the Emperor of Germany.

Ambush II, owned by HRH the Prince of Wales, won the Grand National by four lengths in 1900. The skeleton of his horse, the only Royal winner of the Grand National, stands today in the Museum of Liverpool Life at the Albert Dock on the banks of the River Mersey.

A raging blizzard engulfed Aintree on Grand National day in 1901 with such ferocity that the jockeys signed a petition to have the race postponed. The race was run with *Grudon* being declared the winner – thanks to the pounds of butter his trainer had rubbed into his hooves to prevent those areas snow-balling.

Then there was the first woman – Lady Nelson – to win the Grand National with *Ally Sloper* in 1915.

Mirabel's Grand National day celebrity guests over the years had included Tommy Trinder, Billy Cotton, Pat

Smythe, Stirling Moss, Henry Cooper and Gregory Peck, who ran two horses in the big race, to name just a few. In 1964 writer Nancy Spain was on her way to Aintree racecourse to join them when her plane crashed and she was killed shortly before the meeting began.

The Queen Mother used the 'facilities' at Paddock Lodge on one occasion. The cloakroom, a spacious room to the left of the main entrance was always equipped with pristine towels and scented soap but the toilet roll could have come from Mirabel's pre-war hoard. It was a relic of the past lacking in texture and flexibility, and made any visit to the facilities rather unpleasant.

The late King and Queen were present in 1937 when *Royal Mail* won the National. Mirabel's special efforts to help with all the exceptional arrangements in connection with the visit were appreciated by the then Lord Derby who wrote to her:

Dear Mrs Topham: I want to thank you for all the various arrangements you made on my behalf this week. Not only for what you have done but also for the flowers you sent which decorated our luncheon table today. We have brought them home with us with a view to putting them in Her Majesty's sitting room. I think as far as we were concerned the meeting had been an unqualified success and I hope it has equally been the same for you.
Yours sincerely
Derby.

Her favourite horse without a doubt was *Red Rum*. I was by her side when *Red Rum* won the National for the third time. Cheering and waving her racecard she turned to me and said: 'Joan you are witnessing racing history.'

She was friendly with Noel Le Mare, *Red Rum's* owner,

and they often shared a glass of champagne together. He told her he had achieved all three of his ambitions – to marry a beautiful woman, become a millionaire and win the Grand National. She invited Ginger McCain to lunch on the occasion he brought *Red Rum* over to Paddock Lodge to be photographed with Pat, Jim, Topper and herself, in the front garden of the house.

She told me the horse deserved all of its glory with the magnificent achievement of winning the Grand National three times and finishing second twice. He died in 1995 aged 30 years and is buried beside the winning post at Aintree his gravestone engraved with the words:

> *Respect this place, this hallowed ground,*
> *A legend here his rest has found.*
> *His feet would fly, our spirits soar.*
> *He earned our love for evermore.*

Mirabel would have approved of those words and his life-size statue, unveiled by the Princess Royal which has now been incorporated in an entrance garden – part of the Aintree improvement plan – in what was once the parade ring. He always took pride of place as the racehorse she most admired and the only one ever to be invited to Paddock Lodge for a polo mint.

Ginger McCain told me: 'Mirabel Topham was a lady to be respected and possessed the special qualities necessary to help in her battles with the establishment. It was at that time a male dominated industry and it took a strong woman to survive. She had a real affection for Aintree racecourse and was let down by a lot of people.

'At the time of her problems, when Bill Davies could – if it had been left to him – have turned the racecourse into a housing estate, I watched Lords Sefton and Derby – the picture of sartorial elegance and autocracy – standing on the racecourse bank, both very wealthy, who could have done more to help.

'If it had been south of the Thames there would have been more help and money available. Mirabel fought a losing battle. Noel Le Mare and myself had a lot of respect for her. She was a tremendous character and a very nice lady.'

Red Rum's first appearance on a racecourse was in the Thursby Selling Plate at Aintree the day before the 1967 Grand National. A two-year-old, he dead heated for first place with *Curlicue*.

Mirabel Topham's entertaining was not restricted to Aintree. She entertained in grand style at her three-storey London home. However, her title of a supreme hostess owed much to the sterling ability in the art of culinary perfection of Pat in her role of chef and general factotum. Mirabel set the scene based on the contents of her blue leather memorandum book to recall the food preference of each guest and what had been served to them on a previous occasion. If a guest had then brought a gift she would make sure it was on view, either on her person, or displayed in the room. She was extremely thoughtful.

There was spontaneous warmth in her welcome and she had a natural talent for making each guest feel appreciated.

Before a party, she and Pat would note down the food to be prepared and served. The choice was overwhelming out of the hundreds of recipes and ideas Mirabel had filed away. Each of the five courses would be planned to the last detail and Pat instructed to order all the food fresh and of quality from the local tradesmen, or by a personal visit, to ensure perfection. Jim would be next to be summoned, and, notebook in hand he would jot down Aunt's requirements for the list of wines to accompany each course.

Blue hydrangeas topped her list of favourite flowers. It was also a shade of blue used in the décor of her London home. The blue carpet in the hall continued up the stairs, with a lighter blue dado around the hall and staircase.

The drawing room was a restful combination of deep soft comfortable seating, and antique furniture, within a colour setting of pastel hues. Before taking her seat at the head of the dining table, Mirabel had already inspected for correctness the place settings of the silver, and the crystal glasses.

On one particular day, there was a starter of melon laced with port, followed by consommé, a third course of halibut in creamy cheese sauce, the main course, roast sirloin of beef (a special order of sirloin undercut) new and roast potatoes, Yorkshire pudding, a selection of fresh vegetables, followed by a choice of fruit salad, damson pie, crème caramel and chocolate éclairs. For the guest with an elasticised stomach there was a choice of cheeses, including ripe Stilton, grapes and celery. Coffee and liquors, and to finish a glass of brandy with a Havana cigar.

At the Queen Bee's dinner parties gentlemen were not given the opportunity to enjoy their own company, male conversation, brandy and cigars, while the ladies withdrew to the drawing room, as was the custom at dinner parties of the era. No one retired anywhere while Mirabel was in charge of protocol – each guest of both sexes was expected to mingle and entertain.

Jim and I enjoyed much hospitality at Paddock Lodge and when we returned their kindness, I made an extra effort to offer a lunch which I hoped they would enjoy, but I could in no way compete with Mirabel and Pat's cordon bleu skills. Mirabel and my husband Jim had bonded on their first meeting. They were two of a kind, plain speaking with no pretence, always telling the truth without fear or favour and in my husband's case with no diplomacy whatsoever.

For example, departing and appreciating Mirabel's usual high standard of hospitality at Paddock Lodge, I expressed my thanks and as I often say to friends: 'You must come over and have lunch with us.' Mirabel smilingly nodded then Jim interrupted: 'Don't make it too soon because we have said all we have to say.' Fortunately, Mirabel roared with laughter, and her nephew told me afterwards, that his Aunt was still chuckling an hour later and told him: 'You know Jim, he is right.'

For one lunch party at Lower Alder Root Farm, I tried to include guests who would be of interest to the Topham Trio, who always brought along Topper! Tom Dawson, the *Daily Express* Northern racing correspondent who wrote under the name of 'Sir Harry', and his wife were a popular choice. Tom was a gentleman of journalism and I knew the Topham family liked and respected him. My sister-in-law, Dr Anne McCandless, a retired paediatrician, was guaranteed to give a 'Lady Pilkington' performance to ignite the conversation with fun and light-hearted discussion.

My hostess present from Mirabel on this occasion was a yard of Bendicks dark chocolate bitter mints, which were my favourites. The conversation and good humour flowed, and I was very flattered at the end of the afternoon, when Pat and Mirabel asked for my recipe for the brandy cream pudding and congratulated me on my culinary skill.

It was indeed a compliment coming from them and my awareness of her sense of humour prompted me to tell her in all honesty of the time early in my marriage when

I took an ingenious short-cut in my food preparation department to compete with a perfect mother-in-law.

My husband's mother had reached the summit of culinary perfection. She could produce individual fruit pies with a pleasurable succulence, which would remain on the palate long after the final bite. Her roasts with all the trimmings and her sponge cakes were renowned.

Throughout the early years of my married life I could never, in my Jim's opinion, cook a meal with the same excellence as his mother. I must say with modesty, that I was a reasonable cook and fast proving a fairly competent farmer's wife. I could pluck and clean a pheasant, skin a hare and remove the inner parts, and what a bloody job that turned out to be.

I prepared ox-tail, rabbit casserole, and lambs' kidneys in mustard and cream, created a blackberry pie from the blackberries I handpicked from the hedgerows. On Christmas Day, in addition to cooking the turkey and all the trimmings, I would sizzle a hundred and fifty pork sausages in preparation for the Boxing Day shoot.

At 7.30 every morning, Jim sat down to a cooked breakfast of egg, bacon, mushrooms, tomatoes, sausage and fried bread.

I would occasionally, in the hope of being rewarded with a rare compliment, ask: 'Now Jim, you obviously enjoyed that – was it as good as your mother's?' He would shake his head slowly and say: 'Joanie, it wasn't bad but you will never cook as good as mother.'

Heaven only knows I really tried hard but it seemed that I was destined to remain second best in the Rimmer culinary stakes. That was until one day a tin of rice pudding – a treat intended for our cat Thomas and tucked away on the pantry shelf – gave me a lead to the accolade.

Rice pudding served with a large portion of fruit

pie and topped with a dollop of double cream was Jim's favourite lunchtime snack.

On this particular day, I had had a busy morning and as lunchtime approached I realised with some consternation, I had forgotten to put a rice pudding in the Aga. Trying desperately to devise an alternative, I suddenly remember Thomas's tin. With a twinge of conscience I opened the tin and emptied the contents into the rice pudding dish. I stirred in a cup of cream, a tablespoon of sugar and sprinkled on top grated nutmeg and nobs of butter. Placing it into the top oven of the Aga, until the butter and nutmeg bubbled into a crisp topping.

Jim arrived five minutes later and I placed before him a large slice of apple pie topped with the cat's rice pudding. I watched with some trepidation as he demolished the lot and then to my surprise asked for seconds.

Beaming with satisfaction he viewed the empty dish. 'My word Joan, that rice pudding was excellent, certainly as good as mother made!' I later wrapped the empty tin in several bags and buried it deep into the bottom of the refuse bin. That was going to be my little secret until I shared with Mirabel and Pat and they thought it hilarious.

Late spring, the Topham Trio and Topper would travel to their summer residence on the Isle of Wight to recharge their batteries. It was a haven of peace after all the hectic activity of Aintree and the surfeit of entertaining while in London.

We had been invited to join them there on a number of occasions but Jim was reluctant to travel so far and there was always the harvest to worry about.

A year after Mirabel's death, Pat and Jim extended to us another invitation to stay a week with them at Seaview and this time we accepted, although my Jim, a typical farmer, was at first reluctant.

He had never been abroad, had no wish to do so and we rarely went on holiday. The extent of our journeying in pursuit of relaxation had been a drive to Scotland, or a long weekend at Trearddur Bay, Anglesey, where his brother Bill and wife Honor had a holiday home.

If the sun shone and all was safely gathered in, he would say: 'Come on Joanie let's go for a drive and see what the other farmers are up to!' It was a nightmare of an outing. I nervously sat next to him, my right foot constantly dipping on an imaginary brake as he motored, as if, by remote control, along the lanes, his eyes focused to the right surveying the farm fields. Fortunately in those days there was little traffic to worry about.

Even the suggestion of a few days away for a honeymoon after our wedding on March 22nd 1957, had no appeal. In fairness we had just bought the 140-acre arable farm, latterly neglected by Winwick Mental Hospital, and there was much to do in preparing the land for the crops we were hoping to grow. En route after the wedding reception, we dined at a hotel before making our way to the farm.

The electricity had yet to be connected so it was bitterly cold and pitch dark. The only warmth came from the solid fuel Aga cooker in the kitchen, a wedding present from my parents. Jim lit some candles – we had decided against oil lamps which might discolour our new paintwork. We had a cup of tea, crouched over the Aga jostling for the best heating position with our dog and the farm cat we had inherited from the previous occupants.

Having thawed out sufficiently to brave the cold blast we hurried upstairs to disappear under a hillock of blankets, eiderdowns, Jim's dufflecoat and the dog! It was not the most romantic of nights. Jim was worried about all the work he had to catch up on and that he had to be up at the crack of dawn to get on with it. We fell asleep holding hands with my icy toes luxuriating in the warmth of his feet.

The morning after our wedding, I awakened at 7 a.m. and turned towards Jim's side of the bed. There was a hollow where his head should have been, blue and white striped pyjamas were neatly folded but he was nowhere to be seen. I pulled on my warm dressing gown and ventured forth into the freezing cold to scan the land from all the windows. In the distance, I spotted the tractor, Jim at the helm full of energy and enthusiasm in his quest to till our good earth.

I recalled one of the many greetings telegrams sent by *Daily Express* colleagues on the previous day: 'You marrying a farmer. Come inside. The neighbours.'

The neighbours were, of course, in Winwick hospital!

Mirabel approved of this story – putting work before pleasure.

For a while Jim pondered on Pat and Jim's kind invitation. 'It's a long distance,' he muttered as we studied the map. I suggested we stay overnight halfway before boarding the ferry to the island. He finally agreed and the ride on the ferry was for him as exciting as a world cruise, an adventure remaining with him for years to come.

The sun shone and we were warmly welcomed at the quayside by Jim and Pat. At the house, Nippy greeted her friend Topper rapturously racing around the garden in a frenzy of excitement.

The visit coincided with the wedding of Prince Charles and Diana and to celebrate the occasion Pat had arranged a special luncheon for the four of us. We relaxed on the terrace surrounded by Mirabel's collection of gnomes and after downing the fourth champagne cocktail, the diminutive figures with their cheerful faces seemed to nod their approval.

The terrace, or deck, jutted out and obscured from view the private footpath below leading to the beach and as a consequence it seemed as if we were seated on the deck of a liner with an uninterrupted view of the Solent and the shipping beyond.

We toasted the Royal couple and feasted off a large lobster each with new potatoes, vegetables and raspberries from the garden. In the days that followed we relaxed and explored. Pat and I swam in the sea while my Jim sat on the terrace smoking a large Havana cigar, and with the posture of a ship's captain, gazed out over the Solent.

Jim Topham busied himself in Mirabel's large stately house at the top of the hill. He was always busy in which ever of their three homes they happened to be and we never did find out what kept him so occupied.

We stayed in the sprawling dormer bungalow and you could understand why Mirabel had so enjoyed her holidays there. We all missed her company but Jim's recollections of 'dear Aunty' meant that she was often in our thoughts.

The two Jack Russells played continuously on the beach, Topper growling at any dog daring to come within a tail-wag distance of his friend.

We saw several shows, enjoying the typical end-of-the-pier raucous humour. During the day Pat and Jim drove us around the island. On one occasion we lunched at a pleasant Country Club and Hotel owned by Fred Pontin whose horse *Specify* had won the Grand National in 1971.

On that occasion my Jim had backed it as an outsider and won a large amount of money. To our surprise and delight, *Specify*, enjoying a well-earned retirement, was grazing in the field next to the hotel.

The time passed quickly and we both had enjoyed a superb holiday and generous hospitality. For farmer Jim it was his best holiday ever. Indeed, when the day came for our return he pondered to me on the possibility that we might be able to stay a few extra days.

Definitely not. I refused even to enquire, remembering Mirabel's story of husband Ronald's nephew Mark who came to stay for two nights and nine days later was still in residence. Mirabel gave him a sharp reminder that he had overstayed his welcome and he departed hastily 'with a flea in his ear,' never to be invited again.

CHAPTER SEVEN

THE FINAL CURTAIN

Mirabel Topham happily acknowledged that she was not the most popular person on the racing scene. Criticism of her attitude, obstinacy and bullying was renowned and in a way she quite enjoyed this disapproval. It gave her an aura of strength and authority and the extra muscle to bandy words with whosoever she dealt.

In the early days there were those who said she had married into the prestigious Topham racecourse family to establish herself in a more important role than that of an actress. She must have been aware at the time of their courtship of the many weaknesses of her future husband and yet was still brave and confident enough to marry him.

But say what you will about Mirabel, she truly loved Aintree racecourse and its famous race, and any marital disharmony which existed between her and Ronald Topham was a price she never regretted having to pay.

It would be interesting to hear Mirabel's opinion of the massive amount of money now available and being spent on her much loved racecourse. She was parsimonious to the extreme, and in her sewing room at Paddock Lodge, clothes were patched, Jim's socks darned and his best shirts had their collars turned for further use. Even the magnificent plumage adorning the brims of her famous collection of hats was recycled to grace headwear worn on another occasion.

She would not have been agreeable with some aspects

of the £34 million redesign of Aintree racecourse today – in particular the relocation of the parade ring, winner's and unsaddling Enclosure and the building of a new weighing room and stable complex which assigned a part of her era into history.

However, I am sure that she would have been pleased that the name of Topham – synonymous with Aintree for a total of 158 years – has been entwined for eternity in its golden future as a racecourse worthy of being the setting for the world's greatest steeplechase.

It deserved a second chance when its future was so uncertain in the early 1960s. Mirabel, with problems of time, energy and money, and a heavy heart, decided it was time to sell. The decision of Bill Davies, a property company developer – now living in Monaco – to buy seemed to presage the end of the racecourse and with it the most famous steeplechase in the world.

While the lawyers wrangled, each successive Grand National was forlornly expected to be the last. The course was finally sold to Bill Davies in 1973 and it was in that year that the National saw one of its greatest-ever runnings when *Red Rum* caught the front-running *Crisp* in the shadow of the post to register his first National triumph.

Bill Whittle, who succeeded his father the late Thomas Whittle, a highly respected chairman of Haydock Park racecourse, told me:

'They were dark days and it was all hands on deck. Aintree was dropping to bits and Haydock went to the rescue with the loan of staff, running rails and even lead weights and helped wherever we could. Somehow the course refused to die, and in 1975 bookmakers Ladbrokes leased the course from the new owners for seven years – thus allowing *Red Rum* his glorious third National victory in 1977. When that lease expired in 1982 the Jockey Club launched a public appeal for funds to save the home of the Grand National, and although the full sum of approximately £3 million was not realised, Bill Davies agreed to accept a lower figure and Aintree was saved.

'The trustees of the appeal came to an agreement whereby ownership would pass to the Racecourse Holdings Trust (RHT), now renamed Jockey Club Racecourses, with the Aintree Racecourse company being established to run the course. Mirabel had died two years previously and was never to see the remarkable transformation from down-at-heel, cheerless racecourse in the 1970s surviving on the rapidly fading glory of its famous race, to the well-appointed modern racecourse it is today.

'The place buzzes with excitement not just on National Day, but through the whole of the revitalised spring meeting and the restored autumn fixture which features the Becher Chase.'

Mirabel must have reflected at some time on the advantage of a lifeline from the Racecourse Holdings Trust, thus shortening the period of uncertainty, anxiety and the nine year drawn out saga of the sale of Aintree racecourse, but the price in those early days would not have been right or such a large sum of money available. She wanted Aintree to remain an independent racecourse and had hoped that a private buyer would continue where she had left off.

In addition she would have been reluctant to have sought help from the Establishment with which she had crossed swords on a number of previous occasions. She passed away not knowing that her beloved racecourse would be indebted for its golden future to the Jockey Club Racecourses and in the end she would have had to bury the hatchet.

Bill Whittle continued: 'An astute businesswoman, who kept her fingers on the pulse of every aspect of the racecourse business, she would have been well aware of all the preliminary discussions of the Racing Reorganisation Committee back in 1943 on the takeover on fair terms of a selected number of racecourses, thereby guaranteeing them a more stable future.

'She would have noted with interest in 1964 the creation of RHT and the success of its first venture at such a prestigious course as Cheltenham. What she did not know from her prolific reading of everything concerned with racing, she would have learned from nephew Jim who absorbed racecourse intelligence from whichever source, to pass on to her.

'They were a great team and she once told me – rather unkindly, I thought at the time – "Jim has all the brains and a photographic memory and Pat is superb in the kitchen."

'Members of the Jockey Club were entertained in some style for luncheon at Paddock Lodge and it is more than likely that between courses, which usually included "succulent roast-beef", so described by one member, that she would have interrogated them about the business of RHT.

'She could be a stubborn woman, fiercely independent, anti-establishment and a sharp business manipulator. As such she was determined to find the highest bidder for Aintree no matter what.

'Seven racecourses Cheltenham (1964), Wincanton (1966), Nottingham and Warwick (1967), Market Rasen (1968), Newmarket (1974) and Haydock (1978) were taken over before Aintree in 1982. Mirabel had died two years previously and never witnessed the takeover, which brought to the course she regarded with so much affection, a new lease of life beyond her most fanciful dreams.

'Time would reveal that had the other reluctant rescuers put forward their money to save Aintree racecourse, it could have proved an admirable future investment. A number of people made a lot of money by selling their shares at a premium when the Jockey Club sat in the pilot's seat and moved forward to revolutionise some of the country's racecourse businesses. Racecourse Holdings Trust Ltd began life in a very modest way.

'Maintaining racecourses as viable commercial ventures had been a concern of racing authorities long before the formation of the Racecourse Holdings Trust in 1964 – the year Mirabel, at the age of 72, decided to sell Aintree.

'In 1943, a report by the Racing Reorganisation Committee of the Jockey Club revealed that only a small minority of courses did not pay dividends to shareholders, preferring to invest profits in course improvements. The committee declared that courses should be run in such a way that any trading surplus would be put back into racing and were of the opinion that something could be arranged on those lines. Their idea was to acquire on fair terms the control of a selected number of racecourses, which would be taken over.'

At the time they assessed what would be needed to operate such an undertaking, and were satisfied that it could be adapted to the present system of horse racing. This was in fact the substance of the idea which laid the foundation of RHT – but it would be over 20 years later before it became a reality.

By 1964 the rate at which racecourses were closing – for several reasons – was on the increase, with some courses feeling insecure about their future.

The owners of Hurst Park – a major track for both flat and National Hunt racing – decided in 1962 that there was more money to be made from selling the land to property developers than keeping it as a racecourse. They feared the long-term effect on attendance of recently opened High Street betting shops.

Another major course made its final exit when Manchester staged its last meeting in 1963. There were nine racecourse closures in the space of six years. It was Cheltenham, the country's leading National Hunt course that brought the RHT plans into being.

In March 1964 Cheltenham staged one of the greatest races in steeplechasing history, the epic Gold Cup won by *Arkle* at the expense of *Mill House* but at the time of celebration the directors were aware of the urgent need to upgrade the course facilities – notably the provision of a new weighing room.

Ruby Holland-Martin, a director of the Steeplecourse Company (Cheltenham) Ltd, the private company which owned the course, approached Johnny Henderson (father of trainer Nicky Henderson) at the stockbrokers Cazenove about holding a rights issue among the shareholders to finance the scheme.

Not all the shareholders were able to support the issue, and to prevent shares getting into the wrong hands with the risk of the course being bought by developers, a plan was devised to buyout all the shareholders and place the shares in a non-profit-making trust – to be named the Racecourse Holding Trust – which would preserve Cheltenham as a racecourse in perpetuity.

It was launched as a holding company, run by Johnny Henderson from his office at Cazenove and with an original capital base of £1,700 in the form of 1,700 ordinary shares held by 17 individuals who felt so strongly about the survival of Cheltenham that they agreed that no dividends would ever be paid. The course changed hands for just £240,000 – considerably less than the prize money for the 2007 Gold Cup – that sum being financed in part by a loan from insurance companies and guaranteed by the Horserace Betting Levy Board – the organisation set up to collect the levy from bookmakers following the opening of betting shops – and partly by bank loans.

RHT was in business. Purchasing the Cheltenham Steeplechase Company and ensuring its long-term future, which would include a rolling £60 million programme of redevelopment, was initially the sole objective of RHT, but before long other racecourses were seeking their help.

They were: Aintree, Haydock Park, Carlisle, Cheltenham, Epsom Downs, Huntingdon, Kempton Park, Market Rasen, Newmarket, Nottingham, Sandown Park, Warwick, Wincanton and Exeter (in 2007).

Group revenue from racing in 2005 – the 2006 figures are not yet available – amounted to £63.1 million, with a further £11.6 million contributions from non-racing events and leisure activities. Arena Leisure run seven other racecourses and Northern Racing are responsible for nine.

From 2002–06 Racecourse Holdings Trust invested over 120 million in capital expenditure projects. Profits generated by major courses such as Cheltenham and Aintree are reinvested across the group and this has enabled smaller courses to redevelop and grow in a way that would not have been possible had they remained independent. Boards are accountable for the governance of their individual business and for local management of their racecourse.

The company encourages more local directors of these boards. Andrew Coppel, the chief executive explained:

'We assess all future capital projects carefully, prioritise them and invest where we identify the greatest long-term benefit to the course and to the racing industry as a whole. We are committed to maximising the revenue-generating potential of our considerable assets and are actively seeking new opportunities to develop our courses as attractive events and leisure centres of excellence in racing.

'Our overall objective is to be the best racecourse operator in the world in terms of profitability and the promotion of the best flat, jump and AWT racing experience, and to establish our racecourses as venues of choice in the UK conference and events markets.'

They have certainly provided the means for the revitalisation of courses with uncertain futures.

Projects costing £31 million due for completion at Aintree include a new grandstand complex and an international equestrian centre with a parade ring and two bandstands which were unveiled at the 2007 John Smith's Grand National meeting.

There are vastly improved facilities for jockeys at Aintree. The changing area will have space for up to 80 male jockeys and in a separate room, space for 10 female jockeys.

Horses too, will benefit from further investment in equine facilities including the building of a new stable block, which will incorporate a state of the art veterinary treatment facility and a modern dope-testing unit. A new pre-parade ring will have 26 new saddling boxes built around the outside.

Aintree in suburban Liverpool – unlike Haydock a course situated in what was once parkland – may not be the most scenically sited course in the country, but as home of the Grand National it has an unrivalled history observing some of the greatest heroics, equine and human, in all sport. Horses have to successfully jump a total of 30 fences.

Each of the 16 individual fences are jumped twice, apart from The Chair and The Water Jump. The race comprises two circuits of the course. Becher's Brook is the sixth fence on the circuit and twenty-second on the second. It was modified for safety purposes in 1989, and remains one of the most formidable fences. It was sad that Aintree had to spend most of its post-war life cowering under the threat of closure.

Mirabel could never have envisaged in her reign as 'Queen Bee' of the racecourse the result of a vast programme of improvement and rebuilding and the provision of so many new attractions and facilities.

There are two new grandstands each providing four tiers of prime viewing, a restaurant overlooking the racecourse for 640 diners, a hospitality suite for 360 diners and six private suites with a vista of the racecourse.

A new entrance to the racecourse will be through 'Grand National Avenue' with panoramic views of all the grandstand areas and the new parade ring. A new Aintree pavilion for Tattersall customers has a public bar, catering, and betting facilities for up to 10,000 racegoers.

Gone are the days when racegoers sought shelter from the driving rain and cold under any type of cover they could find. One really did have to be a race going fan to brave the elements and put up with the discomfort and inadequate facilities.

Today the aim is to provide everyone with a pleasurable day of enjoyment, in warm and agreeable surroundings and with the availability of an excellent choice of food from an extensive menu in restaurants comparable with four-star hotels, to a selection of less expensive food in other areas.

At Haydock Park racecourse which is similarly blessed with the same excellent facilities and ambience, each enclosure offers a wide range of food to suit the taste and finances of all racegoers.

Chairman Bill Whittle told me: 'We have come a long way since the days of Brown Windsor soup and haddock. It is a different game today, what began as watching horses racing is now a pleasant social occasion.'

In her mid-eighties, Mirabel wrote in her blue leather menu book: 'I am very tired.' It was almost as if she was jotting down her concern that perhaps she should take life a little easier.

The earlier attack of shingles, painful and unpleasant, had taken its toll on her energy and wellbeing and she was never quite the same afterwards. Jim and Pat gave her every care, nothing was too much trouble and she had every reason to be grateful for their loyalty, love and attention.

Pat told me: 'Aunt still bosses us but we love her and would do anything for her.' With their help she still entertained low-key with occasional visits from close friends.

She observed from her window at Paddock Lodge the activities of the racecourse beyond. Her brain was as sharp as ever but she was losing some of her spark and accepted without judgement much of the racecourse happenings of which she did not always approve.

In her ninetieth year, she was resting for longer periods and for the first time in her life admitted to feeling unwell. She had told me once that if your body is in perfect working order it runs smoothly and you feel nothing untoward. She could no longer ignore the nagging pain in her stomach and there were other worrying symptoms which indicated that something was wrong.

A consultant suspected it could be serious and insisted she go into hospital for further investigation. During her lengthy lifespan she had never been a hospital patient. It was an experience she had never visualised and although the word 'panic' was not in her vocabulary, she was nervous about facing the unknown.

I had earlier had a hysterectomy from which I was by then fully recovered. Mirabel had followed my progress with kind concern and as the day approached for her hospital admittance telephoned to ask if I would visit Paddock Lodge and tell her about my experience in hospital.

At Aintree, Pat and Jim greeted me with their usual cordiality and Pat took me upstairs to her Aunt's bedroom which spread over a large section of the first floor. The colour scheme was a cheerful feminine pale rose pink and the mahogany bedroom furniture, including the Queen sized bed, had been painted magnolia. Mirabel was propped up by pillows, her hair was, as usual, immaculate. Pat had lovingly brushed the silver swirls into biddable curls to frame Mirabel's face.

She was wearing a gown of pale hyacinth blue with a matching gossamer shawl around her shoulders. Her twinkly blue eyes had lost none of their sparkle. Nestling into the pink silk eiderdown next to her was Topper the devoted Jack Russell. Pat left us alone.

She was pleased to see me but I could sense her apprehension about a trip into the unknown. I explained as best I could about my hospital experience covering the anaesthetic procedure which would send her into a state of oblivion, the superb nursing care, and the hospital procedure geared to help her get better. She asked a number of questions, which I answered honestly and then we philosophised about many things and life in general.

We both agreed that everyone is born with a life to fulfil rather like a new book with its chapters awaiting content. Some people either through lack of ambition, apprehension, or simply being content with the way things are, fail to grasp their opportunities.

Mirabel had achieved so much as a result of her initiative, hard work, personality and brain power. To be 'Queen Bee' of Aintree was an impressive achievement. She had come a long way since riding *Daisy* on stage at the Gaiety Theatre.

Her superb sense of humour surfaced and we were both chuckling as Pat brought in tea with egg sandwiches, and home-made sponge cake.

Half an hour later I kissed Mirabel goodbye, wished her luck and left Paddock Lodge, not realising that I would never see her again. Having been brought up in an age which commanded respect for ones elders, I had always called her Mrs Topham. As I was leaving the room she said: 'Joan – do call me Mirrie.'

The hospital tests revealed cancer. Loyal to the end, Pat and Jim were united in their decision to bring her home where they would nurse her for as long as necessary. It was heartbreaking for them all. Mirabel was no fool and knew she had not long to live. Pat and Jim tended to her every whim and need. They nursed her around the clock to the point of exhaustion. Jim entertained her with snippets of racecourse news and items of interest from the newspapers. Pat prepared a nourishing diet to tempt her failing appetite, and in between time Mirabel would gaze at the racecourse beyond the tulle curtains, exploring her own treasurable memories.

Her faithful Jack Russell was at her side when she died on May 29th 1980, just three months short of her ninetieth birthday. He licked her hand and was reluctant to leave her. Jim gently lifted him away telling him: 'Granny has gone now.'

Pat and Jim were devastated. The most important person in their lives since the death of their mother had gone. The two of them gently laid their Aunt to rest, clothing her in an elegant brown silk gown traced with pale grey leaves and draped a diaphanous pale grey stole around her shoulders.

Pat carefully brushed the silver curls for the last time before pinning onto her gown the Queen Bee brooch. They watched as the undertaker placed the body in the coffin and secured the lid. There was nothing more they could do for their beloved Aunt. The Queen Bee was at peace. Her bed remained in its entirety over the years until Jim died and her ethereal spirit remained.

Among the many glowing tributes paid to her was one from Lord Leverhulme: 'Mrs Topham was a great friend of mine and I had tremendous admiration for her. I had a lot to do with her over the years and she certainly did a great deal for the Grand National. She played a prominent part in racing before she sold the course, and made her mark without a doubt.'

Reporting on her death *The Times*, June 2nd 1980, described her as one of the turf's most forceful and controversial personalities. 'Mrs Topham will be remembered as a large formidable figure of 18 stone, dressed in tweeds and prepared to stand firmly by decisions, however unpopular.

'She enjoyed the scent of battle and was always ready to champion David against Goliath. Her combative spirit inevitably made her a public figure, and the battles in which she engaged gave the public a picture of a tough, unapproachable and obstinate impresario. Her friends and family remember her "engaging charm and sense of humour".'

It was an epitaph of which she would have approved. Her sense of fun and humour remained with her all of her life. At the time of her wedding in 1922, the chairman of one of the committees on which she served wrote: 'I shall miss you dreadfully at our meetings. You were our youngest and best looking member and I always enjoyed a good laugh with you!'

She was buried next to Ronald in the Topham family grave at the top of the hill at the Franciscan Monastery at Pantasaph, North Wales. Every year on the anniversary of her death Jim and Pat with Topper would motor over to plant primroses on her grave.

According to Jim, Uncle Ronald's parents had 16 children although ten died in infancy and they are buried with their parents in the grave, as are Jim and Pat's great grandfather, grandfather and grandmother, their mother being the Topham link.

After the death of their Aunt, Pat and Jim supported each other as best they could but the emptiness she left behind was immeasurable. Topper helped to fill the gap and the emotional bond between dog and brother and sister was full of fellow feeling. They went everywhere together.

When staying overnight at an hotel, Topper was expected to share the room of either his mistress or master and be provided with the same cuisine served to the guests. He was very well behaved and would remain quietly in his bed until they returned. He never chewed or destroyed a thing and Jim said that on a number of occasions he was better behaved than some of the hotel guests.

The Tophams were known at a number of favourite establishments where the manager was pleased to welcome a well-behaved four-legged guest – plus the extra charge demanded for his dinner and board.

If a hotel ever had the misfortune to refuse his admittance, the manager was quickly and effectively put in his place by a few sharp words from Jim who had mastered his Aunt's verbal ability to reduce the most important of personages to size and indeed to call a spade a shovel.

Brother and sister continued their summer sojourn to Seaview but the magic had gone. They missed the vivacity and humour of Mirabel and her planning to make sure that every moment of their time and energy was filled with tasks, which were often unnecessary.

A year after her death they were pleased to receive an invitation from their special friends Brian and Ruth Moore to join them on the 1981 Brighton Run. Brian and Ruth had entered their 1902 Pannard Lavasa, and Topper was included in the invitation.

It was an early start, with cars leaving at 7.15 a.m. The pleasure and excitement of that day lived up to their expectations but by evening Pat was over-tired and excused her presence at the dinner to follow, retiring early to bed. For some time she had been feeling unusually fatigued and lethargic, yet had difficulty sleeping. She had always been full of energy and no matter how demanding the task, never spared herself hard and strenuous work.

Even her favourite pastime of walking Topper around the racecourse became too much and shortened in pace and distance. She accepted her brother's advice to see a doctor and was admitted to hospital for a thorough check up. She was there for sometime and I visited her, smuggling in a favourite treat of breast of partridge in aspic which with a giggle and a wink of her eye she would hide under the sheet whenever the nurse came into the room.

She missed Topper and craved anecdotal news of his antics. She was bright and chatty, and, like me, unaware of the severity of her illness. It was a shock when Jim telephoned me on March 15th 1982, to tell me that his sister had passed away with adrenal cancer. She was 56.

It was a devastating psychological blow for him, as the Topham family saga seemed to be approaching its conclusion. The valuable contents of the memory-filled house at Hanover Terrace, their London residence for 50 years, had been placed in storage pending Jim's plan to move some of the items into Paddock Lodge.

It was not to be. The huge Cheshire storage depot where they and other items from their Isle of Wight homes had been deposited was burned out and few of Mirabel's precious items survived the fire.

As time moved on, Jim no longer wished to travel to the Isle of Wight. The inspiration had gone and the loneliness of both houses there depressed him. The journey too, was tiring and he had begun to experience severe arthritic pains in both hips. The two houses on the island and the remainder of the lease of Hanover Terrace were sold and Paddock Lodge became his permanent home.

After the deaths of Mirabel and Pat, Jim's affection, care and protection of Topper bordered on the obsessive. He recounted anecdotes giving the Jack Russell almost human qualities. He talked to him frequently and each evening as he listened to some ancient ballad on the gramophone, Topper would be on his knee, head resting on master's arm.

Little did Mirabel realise when she paid with her pension for the small, insignificant Jack Russell – 'my pension pup' – that he would finish up proving an important means of solace to all of them and in particular the last remaining member of her trio.

The Christmas following Pat's death, we invited Jim and Topper to join our family Christmas. We had previously enjoyed generous hospitality when regularly invited to Paddock Lodge for their pre-Christmas lunch.

After a delicious meal, there would be presents under the large, decorated Christmas tree for us all, including gifts for the two Jack Russells. It was always the happiest of occasions.

Jim had already met and liked the members of the Rimmer family who always joined us on Christmas Day, and was happy to accept rather than spend it alone at Paddock Lodge. He came for a number of years, staying overnight in our guest room so that he could indulge in the champagne and not drive home. The Christmas festivities seemed to help distract him if only briefly from his loneliness. I have a photograph of him relaxed in the armchair, Topper on his knee, a large cigar between his fingers and smiling broadly.

My husband died in 1991 and the following Christmas I told Jim that if he so wished he was welcome to continue to join our Christmas party and use the guest room to avoid the drive back to Aintree that night.

The continuing influence of Aunt was evident in his reply: 'It is immensely kind of you Joan, but Aunt once told me that if a gentleman stays overnight under the same roof of a lady living alone it could sully her reputation.' By this time poor Jim was partly crippled with the arthritis. He could drive, but for mobility needed a stick and occasionally a Zimmer frame. I smiled inwardly doubting if he could have mounted my bed never mind my body without falling flat on his face... even if I had wanted him to do so, which I certainly did not.

He continued to come over with Topper for a Sunday lunch and I always invited a few friends whom I knew he liked and found interesting. A favourite was Howard Bygrave, northern editor of the *Sunday Express*, and his wife Rene. Howard was guaranteed to 'sing for his supper' with snippets of titillating news from the London desk or news of celebrities that never made the headlines in those day.

It is surprising now, to reflect that 50 years ago, a person who had already given a story to a newspaper, could telephone their change of mind about publication, and if time allowed this would be honoured by the editor. The reporters of that era were expected to dress with a degree of decorum and I recall one male journalist being sent home to replace the cravat he was wearing, with a tie.

Howard, in the early days, had shared a flat with John Gordon whose *Sunday Express* column had a great following. They had remained firm friends over the years and the behind-the-scene stories he passed on to Howard were often worthy of another hearing, particularly by an appreciative Jim Topham, who was always amused by Howard's flair for a descriptive phrase: 'Ted Heath is like a neutered Tom!' The other guests often included a gynaecologist and his wife, friends of long standing.

His stories were naughty but most entertaining. Jim enjoyed medical stories of any description and would listen in fascination as the consultant rattled off another anecdote of his latest professional encounter.

This will amuse him, I thought, having heard the story before and fairly sure of what was to follow. Jim poised, a piece of roast lamb on the end of his fork a few inches from his mouth and gazed in high expectation towards the storyteller.

'I had a patient the other day who said to me "Doctor I rarely have sex". I looked up and nodded understandingly, having already noted that she had a vagina like the Mersey Tunnel.' The morsel of lamb plummeted to the plate as Jim mentally probed the anatomical significance of the anecdote before roaring with laughter.

For several years after the deaths of his Aunt and sister, Jim organised his own Grand National parties at Paddock Lodge, for a small circle of close friends. Brian, Ruth, Jim and I were invited on both the Friday and Saturday of the meeting. With the help of caterers, our host made an effort to provide cuisine comparable to his Aunt's special brand of hospitality – champagne, a buffet of smoked salmon, lobster, potted shrimps, salad and new potatoes, followed by raspberry pavlova. The white wine had been ordered from an Isle of Wight vineyard, and the smoked salmon came from another source there. He had reserved seats in the stands and we were given racecards.

The luncheon parties were held in the former boardroom and at that time the parade ring was so situated that the jockeys and their mounts passing by just beyond the white tulle curtained windows could be watched unobserved. On one occasion Princess Anne rode by before taking part in one of the preliminary races to the National.

They were pleasurable days, we all enjoyed the company and for Jim it provided the opportunity to turn back the clock. The last party was in 1993, but by this time Jim's health had worsened and Paddock Lodge was becoming his refuge from the outside world.

Topper's death at the age of 14 burdened him with additional emotional heartache. His four-legged companion was buried with his predecessors – four Scottie dogs and Becher, the Jack Russell. By the late nineties Jim's health had seriously deteriorated in spite of having a heart bypass operation in 1991 and one hip replaced in 1996.

The pain of the arthritis in his other hip and knees was agonising and his journeying beyond the racecourse became limited. Aunt's indoctrination that pills are no good for you prevented him easing his suffering with prescribed medicines. Instead he tried unsuccessfully various quack methods of dieting in an effort to relieve the pain. When he could no longer drive a car – a pastime which had given him so much pleasure – he used a local taxi-driver, with a car so designed to make it possible for him to enter, be seated and transported as comfortably as possible, on short journeys.

Towards the end of his life, the taxi-driver went alone weekly to the local Sainsbury's with the same itemised shopping list Jim had used for years.

The combination of the loss of Topper – the severance of the last Topham bond – his lack of mobility and torturous pain, left Jim bordering on depression. He became more and more withdrawn and told me several times: 'I have no quality of life to make my existence worth living.'

He no longer came over to lunch at the house but we would meet very occasionally for lunch at a local hotel. The taxi-driver would park as near to the front entrance as possible and I would keep out of sight to avoid Jim's embarrassment as the driver manhandled the bent, crippled figure from car to front door and into the foyer.

I was shocked at the sight of my friend shuffling in with great difficulty, using his failing strength to guide the Zimmer frame in the right direction. Always a gentleman, bordering on Edwardian gentility, he would remove his hat, kiss my cheeks, hand me an orchid, and apologise profusely for 'being an old crock'.

During the meal he retold all the stories of Aunt, Pat and Topper, I had heard before. I gave him my full attention knowing how important it was for him to explore the past to cope with the misery of the present.

His last special outing was on his eightieth birthday

when Brian and Ruth Moore and I invited him to dine at a hotel in Frodsham. He was at first reluctant to accept, stressing his inability to move around without difficulty. In the end he decided to come.

We were old friends, he knew us well and was at ease in our company. As it happened it was the last occasion on which we were all together and for Jim his last pleasurable venture outside the racecourse. We were all saddened as he entered the room guiding his Zimmer frame towards us, pausing to grunt in suffering at every painful manoeuvre.

Ruth and I were presented with an orchid each, and we raised our glasses to toast in champagne Mirabel, Pat and Topper, and all the happy memories of the Grand National meetings we had enjoyed in the past.

At Paddock Lodge, his failing limbs could no longer negotiate the stairs nor the extent of the rambling house. The log fires had long since gone and he slept, ate and lived in the kitchen, warmed by a Dimplex and electric fire. Once a week he would telephone me for a chat which usually lasted an hour. All his memories were of Aunt, Pat and Topper, every story steeped in nostalgia and the musings of a very unhappy old man. To Jim the past was always more comforting than the present.

The bicycle he rode as a young boy still remained propped up in the garage behind the house. It was a committal to the memory of his much loved mother who provided the love and support for him and his sister when their father died.

He lost interest in Paddock Lodge, and hardly noticed the sad fact that it had fallen into a state of disrepair. The roof leaked and dripped water into Mirabel's pink bedroom and a combination of mice, moths and damp had taken its toll on some of her clothing. He had neither the agility nor incentive to find out what was happening upstairs, and had become obsessive about his privacy.

His favourite treat had been pheasant in aspic and pickled beetroot. I had often prepared this for him, which he greatly enjoyed. I was surprised one day, when, during our lengthy chat, he asked as a favour, if I could do it for him. I was pleased to oblige and followed his instructions that it must be left at the racecourse office for collection, as he did not want anyone coming to the house.

The boardroom where Mirabel had entertained members of the Jockey Club for a pre-National glass of champagne was musty and layered with dust. Jim entered only to use the telephone in the corner of the room. His unhappiest times were at Christmas and during the Grand National meeting. On these days he drew the curtains, locked the door and went into hiding, under the pretence of being away. He never answered the doorbell, not that anyone ever called any more.

An earlier suggestion that rather than sleeping in a chair in the kitchen he might be more comfortable if a bed, with the head facing the door, could be manoeuvred into a space in the cloakroom, brought a sharp reply: 'Not a chance. I am not sleeping there. Aunt said if you sleep in a bed facing the door you are on your way out.'

He had little interest in the activities of the racecourse beyond, although upset by much of their plan for a £30m redevelopment and modernisation enterprise to further increase profits. Large-scale areas were being used for corporate entertaining and conferences, weddings, christenings, private parties and even hospitality after funerals can now be held there.

It is a sombre tribute, but a number of patrons of both Aintree and Haydock racecourses have made requests in their wills or on their death-beds that their ashes be scattered on the courses where they had enjoyed so much pleasure. At Haydock one asked that his ashes be spread under the trees at the six-furlong starting gate, a 'beauty spot', he wrote in his will, 'I have admired for years.'

It is big ever-increasing business and some of the innovative ideas would have sent Aunt spinning in her grave. Jim's deepest hurt, and what he considered was the nail in her coffin, was the demolition of the racecourse's historic weighing room and winner's enclosure.

The latter, a listed building had been in use since 1858. The weighing room itself is thought to have been in place even before the Grand Liverpool Steeplechase in 1839.

However, the historical starting bell which had been in use since the Grand National began has been given to the racecourse for its continued contribution to Aintree history.

Latterly, alone with his ghosts and overwhelmed by pain and despondency, Jim found the distant reverberation of excitement from his last Grand Nationals irritating and intrusive. The laughter, clatter and the horses' part of the vibrant scene beyond were of no importance or interest to the former clerk of the course.

At the beginning of 2005, his health went into severe decline. During the previous year he had collapsed on the kitchen floor and in spite of his protests had been admitted to the Sefton General Hospital. He spent two months there before returning to Paddock Lodge, refusing a home assessment and saying he could manage very well. This was not to be and he was readmitted to the National Health hospital in mid-October.

His authoritative attitude towards patients and staff was accepted with good humour by the Liverpudlians on the public ward and they nicknamed him 'Lord Topham'. He died of acute renal failure in the early hours of Thursday, November 18th, 2005 aged 82. He was buried in a family grave with his mother and sister, overlooking the Malvern Hills in Worcester. The monks at the Franciscan Monastery at Pantasaph were asked to say prayers on his behalf.

James Christopher Howard Bidwell-Topham was always something of an enigma partly because of his Aunt's influence. In his lifetime he had contributed a large monthly sum into a Private Health Insurance scheme. It seemed illogical that being such a private person he should spend so much time in a National Health ward when he could have so easily enjoyed the privacy and comfort of private health care. When asked why? He replied; 'I am saving it for a rainy day.'

EPILOGUE

Charles Barnett, then managing director of Aintree told me: 'The last of the old Aintree has been pulled down or repaired. Today, it is much easier to plan for a bright future and set the plan in motion with support and enthusiasm to provide an exceptional venue for the racing public. We now have the freedom to move forward – the old racecourse was stuck in the past.'

After the deaths of Mirabel and Pat, Charles Barnett and Lord Daresbury, the chairman of Aintree racecourse and a director of Jockey Club Racecourses, continued to offer the hand of friendship to Jim, the last remaining member of the Topham family on site. Said Charles Barnett: 'In the early days we often had lunch together and Lord Daresbury would invite Jim to his home near Warrington for dinner.

'At one of the dinner parties, he and his wife tried to cheer up Jim by inviting as a fellow guest the very attractive celebrated Badminton three-day eventer Lucinda Prior-Palmer to partner him for the evening. They chatted with some animation but that was it. Sadly towards the end of his life Jim became very reclusive and we saw nothing of him any more. It was all very sad.'

Charles Barnett left Aintree racecourse in May 2007 after 15 successful years as its chief executive to take up a role as chief executive at Ascot. His successor at Aintree was Julian Thick.

ABOUT THE AUTHOR

Joan Rimmer is a former *Daily Express* journalist with a particular interest in research. She is a retired Warrington magistrate of nearly 20 years service and was awarded the BEM in 1990 for Services to the Community.

Her previous book is *Yesterday's Naughty Children*, the history of the Liverpool Juvenile Reformatory Association which was founded in 1855.

She married a farmer with a keen interest in racing who attended all the Haydock Park and Aintree meetings up until his death.